"From luxury brands to art collaborations, from pos[...] Federica Carlotto deftly analyzes the contemporary luxury imaginary. She produces useful and accessible insights into art's co-operative manifestations and surveys numerous theoretical and practical approaches to postmodern consumer culture."

John Armitage, *University of Southampton*

"In this highly original study, the case studies chosen are rich and their analysis within the framework of postmodern consumer culture is compelling. The varied approach to the entangled notion of luxury and art enriches our understanding of a phenomenon that will have an impact on current and future discourses, both high and low."

Flavia Frigeri, *Art historian and curator*

"Essential reading! *Luxury Brand and Art Collaborations: Postmodern Consumer Culture* provides a provocative analysis in a fresh approach to understanding how art and luxury are entwined in a post-modern, experiential and digitally networked world. The book provides theoretically nuanced insights into how place-making, time-work and social status redefinitions are triggered by the management of collaborations between artists, creative directors and executives of luxury brand corporations. Timely is an understatement!"

Annamma Joy, *Professor of Marketing, University of British Columbia*

"Where does luxury end and art begin? A compelling and illuminating exploration into the true meaning of brand collaborations through a social-cultural lens."

Rebecca Robins, *Global brand and luxury expert, and bestselling author*

Luxury Brand and Art Collaborations

Over the past decades, collaborative initiatives between luxury brands and the art world have been increasing in number and relevance. At first treated as a mere trend or as a marketing stunt, in time luxury-art collaborations have come to be acknowledged as one of the most effective ways luxury brands and artists can position themselves in today's market, engaging with their clients and audiences. This book sheds light on the socio-cultural valence of luxury-art collaborations.

The book explores luxury-art collaborations in the context of postmodern consumption, i.e. as a phenomenon deeply rooted in and emerging from the ways postmodern individuals value and consume objects, contents and ideas. More specifically, the book covers: how collaborations reflect the postmodern condition and liquid consumption practices (hybrid, temporary, hyperreal); the impact of luxury-art collaborations on the evolution of luxury stores and museums, and the emergence of hybrid spaces (art fairs, nomadic exhibitions, pop-up stores) – the temporal features of luxury-art collaborations (short-lived duration and fast-paced tempo) – how luxury-art collaborations reshuffle traditional status dynamics while drawing new boundaries of social distinction based on experience and access – why luxury brands and creatives are redefining their conventional identities, morphing into cultural entities and bricoleurs.

The book appeals to a wide range of readers, from academics and students in art business, luxury studies, consumption behaviour, to professionals in the luxury industry and the art world. The book is also relevant to an international readership of non-specialists interested in current social and cultural matters.

Federica Carlotto is the Programme Director of the Master in Luxury Business at Sotheby's Institute of Art and a social anthropologist specialised in luxury, fashion and other cultural and creative industries. By applying the lens of human science to markets, trends and brands, Federica delves into the thick layers of meaning behind consumer behaviour, producing strategic business intelligence. Her cultural insights also look at connecting business with communities and the society at large, for responsible value creation.

Routledge Studies in Luxury Management

This series explores the luxury industry through an interdisciplinary lens, bringing together cutting-edge research to define and advance this growing field. Contributions to the series present original research from established and emerging scholars across the globe, offering a diverse range of empirical and critical perspectives on the luxury industry. Topics include, but are not limited to, marketing, brand management, sustainability, and supply chain management.

Made in Italy and the Luxury Market
Heritage, Sustainability and Innovation
Edited by Serena Rovai and Manuela De Carlo

Luxury Marketing, Sustainability and Technology
The Future of Luxury Management
Edited by Park Thaichon and Sara Quach

Managing Sustainable Luxury and Digitalization
Technology Trends and Ethical Challenges in the Swiss Luxury Watch
Business
Mario D. Schultz and Peter Seele

Technology and Luxury Hospitality
AI, Blockchain and the Metaverse
Edited by Park Thaichon, Pushan Kumar Dutta, Pethuru Raj Chelliah and Sachin Gupta

Luxury Brand and Art Collaborations
Postmodern Consumer Culture
Federica Carlotto

For more information about this series, please visit: *www.routledge.com/ Routledge-Studies-in-Luxury-Management/book-series/RSLM*

Luxury Brand and Art Collaborations

Postmodern Consumer Culture

Federica Carlotto

Routledge
Taylor & Francis Group

LONDON AND NEW YORK

First published 2024
by Routledge
4 Park Square, Milton Park, Abingdon, Oxon OX14 4RN

and by Routledge
605 Third Avenue, New York, NY 10158

Routledge is an imprint of the Taylor & Francis Group, an informa business

© 2024 Federica Carlotto

British Library Cataloguing-in-Publication Data
A catalogue record for this book is available from the British Library

ISBN: 978-1-032-22770-2 (hbk)
ISBN: 978-1-032-22771-9 (pbk)
ISBN: 978-1-003-27409-4 (ebk)

DOI: 10.4324/9781003274094

Typeset in Times New Roman
by KnowledgeWorks Global Ltd.

To Bruno and Lea

Contents

Introduction

Over the past couple of decades, collaborative initiatives between luxury brands and the art world have been increasing in number and relevance. From a luxury brand management perspective, this is neither unexpected nor peculiar. Since the early 2000s luxury companies have been looking to expand beyond their core business, with the view of strengthening their market share and brand equity. Some have acted alone, such as in the case of Bulgari and Armani branching out into hospitality in 2004 and 2010 (Walid, 2010; Pectu, 2018). Some others have teamed up with partners across sectors in collaborative projects that leverage each other's expertise and reputational cachet: in 2013, car design company Pininfarina signed the box for Chivas Regal's Gold Signature whisky (Shea, 2013); two years later, Hermès tapped into the tech world working with Apple on its latest watch series (Apple, 2015).

In this context, art represented another fertile and promising territory for luxury brands to scout for potential partnerships. Louis Vuitton's creative director Marc Jacobs involved counterculture artist Stephen Sprouse in the design of the Spring/Summer 2001 collection (Oakley Smith and Kubler, 2013). The Louis Vuitton Graffiti bags, with Sprouse's graffiti overwriting the "LV" iconic logo pattern, would pave the way for a series of similar collaborations with other artists and the launch of the Artycapucines Collection in 2019 (LVMH, 2019). In 2006 the French Maison had also piloted Espace Culturel, a format of in-store exhibitions, which would culminate in the opening of the Fondation Louis Vuitton by parent conglomerate LVMH in 2014 (Socha, 2014; Guintcheva, 2015). These activities have both epitomised and popularised the art collaboration as the ultimate extension mode for the luxury industry of the new millennium: since then, numerous brands have engaged with artists, galleries, museums and art foundations, looking for more creative and compelling ways to enrich their portfolio of initiatives.

In assessing the strategic benefits of these collaborations, there seems to be shared consensus among marketing scholars over the fact that, through art, luxury brands are able to elevate the perceived value of their offerings and the engagement level of their customers (Lee, Chen and Wang, 2014; Koronaki,

DOI: 10.4324/9781003274094-1

Kyrousi and Panigyrakis, 2018): this artification process (Shapiro and Heinich, 2012), in other words, helps luxury companies "circumvent the volume
problem" (Kapferer, 2015, p. 63) inherent in their extension, thus mitigating
the risks of brand dilution.

Journalists and analysts in the art sector have instead pointed to the illicit,
almost impure nature of the collaborations between art and luxury – "*liaison
dangereuse*" (The Art Newspaper, 2012) and "love affair" (Burns, 2012).
More generally, this expresses their growing concern for the luxurification
of the art sector, whose players have been adopting the same strategies as the
luxury companies: auction houses rely on marketing-induced hype to drive
the record sales of artworks, and artists like Jeff Koons and Damien Hirst
operate as proper brand powerhouses (Schroeder, 2005; Adam, 2014). As a
result, art ends up being reduced to yet another lifestyle feature: "Once upon a
time, there was a world of difference between a $5,000 drawing and a $5,000
handbag [...]. One belonged to a world of connoisseurship and unique object-
hood; the other was replicable and corporate" (Salmon, 2014, p. 16).

This line of critique rests on and articulates the ontological difference between art and luxury established in the Western tradition, whereby art is conceived to be an "anti-economic" and "disinterested" pursuit (Bourdieu, 1993,
p. 75), whilst luxury belongs to the sphere of utility and commerce, hence
it is somehow mercenary, mundane and ephemeral (Boodro, 1990; Gregory,
2014; McCartney and Tynan, 2021). As a matter of fact, art and luxury do not
exist a priori, nor do they have a specified referent. They sit instead in "an
atmosphere of interpretation" (Danto, in Becker, 2008, p. 149): art is perpetually recreated by the viewer in their act of viewing an object rather than being
an intrinsic property of that object (Wiesing, 2019); similarly, luxury is more
of "a process, an experience rather than a thing" (Berthon et al., 2009, p. 51).
In other words, both art and luxury lie in the eye of the beholder as well as in
the context of shaping that eye's way of seeing (Berger, 2008; Crane, 2012).

This approach to art and luxury as both emergent and situated constructs
invites placing the analysis of luxury brand and art collaborations within the
wider socio-cultural circumstances that determine their nature and appreciation in the first place.

From this perspective, the relationship between art and luxury appears to
be a porous one. In the Western pre-industrial world, for instance, the production of both art pieces and luxury objects pertained to the realm of artisanal work, relying on the craftsman's skilful combination of head and hands
(Sennett, 2009); the same Latin term "*ars* (art)" generally indicated a proper
artwork as well as any other outcome of a practical skill, business or craft
(Lewis, 2023).

Art became a taxonomic indicator in the Renaissance period. In his book
Lives of the Most Eminent Painters, Sculptors, and Architects (1550), art historian Giorgio Vasari established a proper hierarchy of the arts, with painting,
sculpture and architecture appearing at the very top as "major arts", followed by

all the other "minor" or "applied arts": these included a few domains of today's luxury industry, such as jewellery, tapestry and clothing (Hourihane, 2012).

Despite this conceptual and categorical divide, the life and works of artists, artisans and creatives provide countless instances of touchpoints and crossovers. As recalled by jewellery brand Buccellati on their website until 2022, Botticelli, Brunelleschi and Cellini "were goldsmiths before they became sculptors, painters and architects" (Buccellati, 2022). Centuries later, sculptor Alexander Calder would experiment with jewellery producing during his main artistic career more than 1,800 bracelets, necklaces and earrings (Banks, 2016). Fashion designer Elsa Schiaparelli and Surrealist artists shared the same social circles, which inspired Schiaparelli's fashion creations and stimulated Man Ray, André Breton, Salvador Dalí and Max Ernst to include fashion objects in their works, as fashion offered "creative energy" in contrast to "the pretension of the fine arts" (Martin, in Secrest, 2015, p. 64). Roughly in the same years, Coco Chanel worked with Pablo Picasso on the opera *Antigone* (1927) by poet and common friend Jean Cocteau (Chaney, 2012); Cocteau would, in turn, write the manifesto for Chanel's first fine jewellery collection, Bijoux de Diamants (Silver, 2022). Christian Dior started as an art dealer and then moved to fashion design: in 1955, he organised a fashion show at the Musée des Arts Décoratifs in Paris as a preview of an exhibition on 18th-century cabinet makers, the first instance of an haute couture fashion show presented in a museum (Christian Dior, 2020). A keen art collector, Yves Saint Laurent used the body as a three-dimensional canvas to reinterpret the works of Piet Mondrian, Andy Warhol and Pablo Picasso (Rogers, 2019).

While trespassing the boundaries between the two domains, players in art and luxury also had to redraw them repeatedly, alongside human history. Facing the capitalist industrialisation of the 19th and 20th centuries and the integration of mass production into luxury manufacturing, craftsmanship as the proficient use of head and hands evolved into branded excellence (Sudjic, 2009; Boltanski and Esquerre, 2020); on the art front, the mechanised reproducibility of artworks shifted the aesthetic canon from the imitation of nature towards individual expression and unconventional experimentation (Becker, 2008; Benjamin, 2008; Fokt, 2017), spawning intersections with industrial design and advertising (Featherstone, 2007).

The systemic changes and radical transformations characterising the present times represent another defining moment for art and luxury. In today's globalised and digitally networked world, our approach to reality has become increasingly spectacularised, with individuals diverting their focus from the appreciation of the objects' constitutive qualities in favour of the experience objects give them access to (Debord, 1994). In this context, the luxury business and the art sector act like "joint players in a complex aesthetic firmament that together shape and make markets" (Crewe, 2016, p. 518): well-rounded artists succeed in making their message relevant across different channels – including the commercial avenues and social media – while luxury brands are striving to increase their soft power as "mirror[s] of society" (Rambourg, in Gagne, 2021). Besides their immediate business reality, luxury brand and art collaborations thus become the cultural signifiers of "what we need to know about the world we live in and about where the future is going" (Andjelic, 2020).

In alignment with the stance above, this monograph offers a socio-cultural interpretation of luxury brand and art collaborations in the last 20 years. Specifically, these collaborations are here explored in the context of the current consumption culture, i.e., as a phenomenon deeply rooted in and arising from the principles and practices through which societies access, evaluate and consume products – physical and digital objects, contents and ideas – while luxury companies evolve and deliver their value proposition.

The content is organised into five chapters profiling collaborative projects and more spontaneous crossovers between the luxury industry and the art world through a series of dimensions: postmodernity, space, time, status and identity.

After a brief overview on the dimension, each chapter seeks to detail

- how luxury brand and art collaborations reflect the current zeitgeist and its consumption modes across fragmented aesthetics, hybrid categories and hyperreal products
- the impact of luxury brand and art collaborations on place creation, from the convergence between retail and cultural venues to the construction of other commercial heterotopias: satellite events, nomadic exhibitions, pop-up stores, spatial hackings etc.
- the time horizon of luxury brands and art collaborations, tying in our frantic quest for product novelty with the eclectic repackaging of the past and the introduction of new circular consumption's rituals
- the ways luxury brand and art collaborations reshuffle the traditional vocabulary of status, at the same time drawing new boundaries of social distinction based on access and experience
- the evolving role of executives, creative directors and artists in the management and activation of collaborations, which, in turn, shapes the new identity of luxury corporations as cultural advisors and patrons of the arts

The chapters blend in theoretical reflections, scholarly accounts and examples of collaborative initiatives and activations with close-ups on relevant case studies. To keep the text readable and concise, only the most relevant sources have been referenced.

This volume reorganises thoughts and materials that I have gathered during my academic activity at Sotheby's Institute of Art, pioneering the discipline of luxury business and exploring its artistic ramifications.

In assuming complete responsibility for the content and the views here presented, I would like to express my deepest gratitude to my colleagues, students and my exceptional network of experts and practitioners in the high-value industries for their insightful opinions and enduring support. A special acknowledgement to Dr. Steve Priddy and the Routledge editorial team, whose constructive feedback helped me bring this book to fruition.

Bibliography

Adam, G. (2014) "And the first rule is … break all the rules", *The Art Newspaper*, 258, June, p. 15.

Andjelic, A. (2020) "Special report: good collaborations are art, great ones are kitsch", *Highsnobiety*, 13 November. Available at: https://www.highsnobiety.com/p/special-report-what-makes-a-good-collaboration/ (Accessed: 20 January 2022).

Apple (2015) *Apple and Hermès Unveil the Apple Watch Hermès Collection*, 9 September. Available at: https://www.apple.com/newsroom/2015/09/09Apple-and-Herm-s-Unveil-the-Apple-Watch-Herm-s-Collection/ (Accessed: 15 January 2022).

Banks, G. (2016) "Alexander Calder's jewelry is wearable art", *Forbes*, 25 October. Available at: https://www.forbes.com/sites/gracebanks/2016/10/25/wearable-art-alexander-calders-jewellery/?sh=5f7ceab76ad3 (Accessed: 17 January 2022).

Benjamin, W. (2008) *The Work of Art in the Age of Mechanical Reproduction*. Translated by J.A. Underwood. London: Penguin Books.

Becker, H.S. (2008) *Art Worlds*. Berkeley: University of California Press.

Berger, J. (2008) *Ways of Seeing*. London: Penguin Books.

Berthon, P., Pitt, L., Parent, M. and Berthon, J.P. (2009) "Aesthetics and ephemerality: observing and preserving the luxury brand", *California Management Review*, 52/1, pp. 45–66. Available at: https://doi.org/10.1525/cmr.2009.52.1.45.

Boltanski, L. and Esquerre, A. (2020) *Enrichment: A Critique of Commodities*. Translated by C. Porter. Cambridge: Polity Press.

Boodro, M. (1990) "Art and fashion: a fine romance", *ARTnews*, 89/7, pp. 120–127.

Bourdieu, P. (1993) *The Field of Cultural Production: Essays on Art and Literature*. Cambridge: Polity Press.

Buccellati (2022) *Timeless Beauty*. Available at: http://uk.buccellati.com/en/timeless-beauty (Accessed: 17 January 2022).

Burns, C. (2012) "Can their love last forever?", *The Art Newspaper*, 241, December, p. 11.

Chaney, L. (2012) *Chanel: An Intimate Life*. London: Penguin Books.

Christian Dior (2020) *"Christian Dior, Designer of Dreams" at the Musée des Arts Décoratifs*, 14 April [YouTube]. Available at: https://www.youtube.com/watch?v=FLWDWzMrkBE&t=332s (Accessed: 17 January 2022).

Crane, D. (2012) "Boundaries", in A. Geczy and V. Karaminas (eds.) *Fashion and Art*. London: Berg, pp. 99–110.

Crewe, L. (2016) "Placing fashion: art, space, display and the building of luxury fashion markets through retail design", *Progress in Human Geography*, 40/4, pp. 511–529. Available at: https://doi.org/10.1177/0309132515580815.

Debord, G. (1994) *Society of the Spectacle*. Translated by K. Knabb. London: Rebel Press.

Featherstone, M. (2007) *Consumer Culture and Postmodernism*. London: Sage Publications.

Fokt, S. (2017) "The cultural definition of art", *Metaphilosophy*, 48/4, pp. 404–429. Available at: https://doi.org/10.1111/meta.12251.

Gagne, Y. (2021) "Welcome to the post-sellout era", *Fast Company*, 7 May. Available at: https://www.fastcompany.com/90628653/welcome-to-the-post-sellout-era (Accessed: 20 January 2022).

Gregory, A. (2014) "Art and fashion: the mutual appreciation society", *The Wall Street Journal*, 28 March. Available at: https://www.wsj.com/articles/art-and-fashion-the-mutual-appreciation-society-1396031035 (Accessed: 20 January).

Guintcheva, G. (2015) "Art and its contribution to business: the case of Louis Vuitton's Espace Culturel", *The Case Study Centre* [Ref. 515-195-1]. Available at: https://www.thecasecentre.org/products/view?id=131120.

Hourihane, C. (ed.) (2012) *From Minor to Major: The Minor Arts in Medieval Art History*. Princeton: Index of Christian Art.

Kapferer, J.N. (2015) *Kapferer on Luxury: How Luxury Brands Can Grow Yet Remain Rare*. London: Kogan Page.

Koronaki, E., Kyrousi, A.G. and Panigyrakis, G.G. (2018) "The emotional value of arts-based initiatives: strengthening the luxury brand-consumer relationship", *Journal of Business Research*, 85, pp. 406–413. Available at: https://doi.org/10.1016/j.jbusres.2017.10.018.

Lee, H.C., Chen, W.W. and Wang, C.W. (2014) "The role of visual art in enhancing perceived prestige of luxury brands", *Marketing Letters*, 26/4, pp. 593–606. Available at: https://doi.org/10.1007/s11002-014-9292-3.

Lewis, C.T. (2023) "Ars", *An Elementary Latin Dictionary*. Available at: http://www.perseus.tufts.edu/hopper/text?doc=Perseus%3Atext%3A1999.04.0060%3Aentry%3Dars (Accessed: 20 October 2023).

LVMH (2019) *Louis Vuitton Artycapucines Collection Invites Six Artists to Revisit the Iconic Capucines Bag*, 7 June. Available at: https://www.lvmh.com/news-documents/news/louis-vuitton-artycapucines-collection-invites-six-artists-to-revisit-the-iconic-capucines-bag/ (Accessed: 29 September 2023).

McCartney, N. and Tynan, J. (2021) "Fashioning contemporary art: a new interdisciplinary aesthetics in art-design collaborations", *Journal of Visual Art Practice*, 20/1–2, pp. 143–162. Available at: https://doi.org/10.1080/14702029.2021.1940454.

Oakley Smith, M. and Kubler, A. (2013) *Art/Fashion in the 21st Century*. London: Thames & Hudson.

Pectu, O. (2018) "Bulgari hotels and resorts, the success behind the jeweller becoming a true luxury hotel brand", *CPPLuxury*, 24 November. Available at: https://cpp-luxury.com/bulgari-hotels-resorts-the-success-behind-the-jeweller-becoming-a-true-luxury-hotel-brand/ (Accessed: 15 January 2022).

Rogers, S. (2019) "7 major ways Yves Saint Laurent changed fashion forever", *Vogue Australia*, 28 July. Available at: https://www.vogue.com.au/fashion/news/7-major-ways-yves-saint-laurent-changed-fashion-forever/image-gallery/ce6f36b39f86267391468d30a0cf54c9 (Accessed: 22 January 2022).

Salmon, F. (2014) "Luxury sets news agenda", *The Art Newspaper*, 258, January, p. 16.

Schroeder, J.E. (2005) "The artist and the brand", *European Journal of Marketing*, 39/11–12, pp. 1291–1305. Available at: https://doi.org/10.1108/03090560510623262.

Secrest, M. (2015) *Elsa Schiaparelli: A Biography*. London: Penguin Books.

Sennett, R. (2009) *The Craftsman*. London: Penguin Books.

Shapiro, R. and Heinich, N. (2012) "When is Artification?", *Contemporary Aesthetics (Journal Archive)*, 4/9. Available at: https://digitalcommons.risd.edu/liberalarts_contempaesthetics/vol0/iss4/9

Shea, E. (2013) "Chivas Regal, Pininfarina flaunt craftsmanship via design partnership", *Luxury Daily*, 28 February. Available at: https://www.luxurydaily.com/chivas-regal-and-pininfarina-flaunt-partnership-with-ultra-luxury-design-for-chivas-18/ (Accessed: 15 January 2022).

Silver, H. (2022) "Chanel marks 90 years of high jewellery with heavenly new necklace", *Wallpaper*, 20 January. Available at: https://www.wallpaper.com/watches-and-jewellery/chanel-high-jewellery-necklace (Accessed: 7 February 2022).

Socha, M. (2014) "The art of Arnault: Louis Vuitton Foundation bows in Paris", *WWD*, 21 October. Available at: https://wwd.com/fashion-news/fashion-features/the-art-of-arnault-7992387/ (Accessed: 15 January 2022).

Sudjic, D. (2009) *The Language of Things*. London: Penguin Books.

The Art Newspaper (2012) "Liaison Dangereuse", *The Art Newspaper*, 241, December, p. 11.

Walid, T. (2010) "Armani opens first hotel in Dubai, plans Milan next", *Reuters*, 27 April. Available at: https://www.reuters.com/article/emirates-armanihotel-idUSLDE63Q1EK20100427 (Accessed: 15 January 2022).

Wiesing, L. (2019) *A Philosophy of Luxury*. Translated by N.A. Roth. London: Routledge.

1   Postmodernity

Throughout the past century, advances in globalisation, the Internet Communication Technologies (ICTs) and a mature capitalistic mode of production
have both extended and accelerated the circulation of people, goods and ideas.
This, in turn, has eroded the political and social institutions, economic structures, systems of knowledge, values and aesthetics on which the modern order
had been conventionally resting, leaving individuals with a fuzzy reality to
make sense of (Bauman, 2000; Appadurai, 2005). The shift has been so profound that certain scholars and critics have coined the term "postmodernity"
to define this new condition of the human existence.[1]

The incessant flow of ideas has called into question the very existence of
transcendental truths and overarching principles, presenting us instead with
a kaleidoscope of partial certainties, conditional impressions, conflicting
viewpoints. It has questioned the human search for any orthodoxy, taxonomy
or narrative above "the contingencies of space and time" (Hughes, 2003,
p. 15). The guiding principle of modernity, i.e., the trust in industrial capitalism, scientific development and technological efficiency as the universal
avenues to progress, has lost its argumentative hegemony, and it has been
relativised as just one viewpoint – Western, white, male – among a plurality of stances from alternative political, economic or socio-cultural entities
(Bauman, 1992; Delanty, 2000). Similarly, the frantic mobility of individuals
travelling across national borders, working with global teams in virtual of-
fices, joining and leaving diasporic families has fragmented that lasting sense
of belonging to nation-states and any other community based on permanent
ties in favour of multiple memberships to loosely networked, temporary forms
of togetherness (Bauman, 1995). Fluctuating in a whirlwind of ideas and relations and without any "game rules" (Lyotard, 1984, p. xxiii) at hand, this class
of postmodern individuals also confronts with the dilution of a stable and
consistent sense of self. In this context, identity is not anymore something we
have, but something we need to build: identity, in other words, turns from a
personal *attribute* into a personal *task* (Holt, 2002).

In contrast to the circulation of people and ideas eroding the political and
social structures of modernity, the flux of products has instead promoted the

DOI: 10.4324/9781003274094-2

market economy into the primary "superstructure" (Bardhi and Eckhardt, 2017, p. 590) of the postmodern era.

Alongside the evolution of the mass media, the social media networks (SMNs) – serving now as both content repositories and retail platforms – and the appearance of non-fungible tokens (NFTs), the marketplace has been flooded by a profusion of physical products, virtual assets, digital contents and images that can be endlessly reproduced and shared (Baudrillard, 2017). While certainly contributing to the loss of stable references, this overabundance of objects has nonetheless reinforced the role of consumption in our postmodern society imbuing it with new connotations. First, consumption has diversified beyond the solid possession of commodities, including additional practices such as the ephemeral access to products and contents (Bardhi and Eckhardt, 2017). Second, the agency of consumers has been further enhanced: more than ever before, it is through the purchase, use and access to material goods as well as cultural materials that individuals communicate their identity, establish social bonds and make sense of the surrounding reality (Holt, 2002). As the main arena where individuals creatively negotiate and generate meanings, the marketplace also becomes "the[ir] sole locus of legitimation" (Firat and Venkatesh, 1995, p. 245): consumption, in other words, comes to exert the "*cognitive* ordering power" (Bauman, 1997, p. 131) that culture used to have in the modern society, yet without any long-term commitment to a specific order, vision of reality or set of values.

Saturated with tangible and digital things and extremely hungry for meanings, consumers engage with objects not in their utilitarian function but as signs, readymade vessels for significance in more complex communicative acts (Baudrillard, 2017): the pipe that is not a pipe portrayed by René Magritte on *The Treachery of Images* (1929) and the 2021 Off-White rain boots with the use instruction "for rainy days" printed on the ankles ironically nod to the postmodern disjunction between the primary function of a product and its symbolic use.

Thus, in their consumption practices the postmodern individual turns from "goods-purveyor" to "sensations-gatherer" (Bauman, 1995, p. 115), looking out for the communicative power of a product rather than from its actual use value. It is from the appearance, or the spectacle, that an object ultimately derives "its immediate prestige and its ultimate purpose" (Debord, 1994, p. 11). In such a highly aestheticised marketplace, the most coveted products are the ones with a spectacle factor, i.e., with original and compelling features or that have been enriched through suggestive narratives and associations (Boltanski and Esquerre, 2020).

From this perspective, luxury brand and art collaborations embody and feed the postmodern search for spectacular consumption.

Spectacular ensembles across genres and styles

By definition, luxury brand and art collaborations stem from the spectacularised juxtaposition of art and luxury.

As the practice to incorporate distinct categories, canons and aesthetics into something novel, juxtaposition consolidated during the 19th and 20th centuries: Dada and Surrealist artworks, the development of advertising and the windows of arcades and department stores mesmerised viewers by presenting collages of heterogenous images, shapes and materials, displaying mundane items together with luxury goods, mixing the commercial and the aesthetic (Benjamin, 1999). Over a very short period, not only would eclecticism be normalised as a proper art form, but it would also come to epitomise the very same spirit of postmodernity: "the universe of the postmodern is not one of delimitation, but intermixture – celebrating the cross-over, the hybrid, the pout-pourri" (Anderson, 1998, p. 93).

In engaging with a plethora of objects on different media platforms, postmodern consumers encounter all manner of juxtapositions: items mixing and matching genres and styles, contents subverting conventional meanings to originate new associations, images recomposed for different contexts of consumption. The resulting hybrid objects are thus endowed with a spectacle factor: by playing with incompatible or unrelated categories, contradictory or unusual codes, opposite or irreverent elements, they present consumers with something unconventional, original and unexpected which, in turn, elicits their surprise and interest.

As mentioned in the introduction, the greatest spectacular attribute of luxury brand and art collaborations lies in and builds on the interbreed between luxury and art, which provocatively questions the received categorisation of the Western tradition. Looking closely at specific collaborative formats, however, it is possible to identify further spectacle triggers.

In product-based collaborations, the artist is usually called to offer a fresh take on a luxury item. The output is a unique piece or a limited edition that captivates attention by interrupting the reproduction of the item in its conventional appearance: this is the case of the Dior Lady Art series and Louis Vuitton's Artycapucines Collection, whereby each year a different line-up of artists reimagines the look of the Lady Dior tote and the Capucines satchel, respectively (LVMH, 2019; Portee, 2021). For wine and spirit brands the opportunity to introduce variation in seriality is offered by the design of labels, bottles and boxes, which usually marks the launch of a new collection: following a 40-year-long roster of artists that includes pop artist Valerio Adami and portrait photographer Annie Leibovitz, in 2021 assemblage artist Sir Peter Blake illustrated the labels for the 13 hand-blown bottles of Macallan Anecdotes of Ages Collection (The Editors of Artnews, 2021); in the same period, Yayoi Kusama reproduced her iconic flower and polka dot patterns on the bottle of the Veuve Clicquot's vintage La Grande Dame 2012 (Pillay, 2021).

Product-based collaborations also present artists with the opportunity to tweak their usual aesthetics on unusual canvases – in terms of size, shape, material. Rolls-Royce, for instance, has equipped its Phantom models with an ad hoc art display feature that goes under the evocative name of The Gallery (Rolls-Royce, 2022). A glass-enclosed space running along the fascia and the panel of the car, The Gallery showcases bespoke art pieces, from the orchid hand-sculpted silk artwork by textile designer Helen Amy Murray (Rolls-Royce Motor Cars Pressclub, 2022) to the geometric motives of the Ndebele group by South African abstract painter Dr. Esther Mahlangu (Rolls-Royce Motor Cars Pressclub, 2020). The façade of the Beaumont hotel in London serves as the architectonic plinth for the three-storey-high, inhabitable sculpture *ROOM* by Antony Gormley: by hosting in its internal cavity a bedroom connected to a suite, *ROOM* "provocatively transcends traditional definitions of art and architecture" (Bruhn, 2016), while also claiming its legitimacy as an in-between art piece and bookable accommodation.

At times, it is the contrast between the size of the artists' signature works and the size of the items they apply their art to that makes for an eye-catching collaboration. Danish-Icelandic artist Olafur Eliasson is usually known for large sculptures and installations: in 2018, he decided to downsize and go bi-dimensional by creating a set of nature-inspired stickers for upscale luggage brand Rimowa (Segran, 2018). Architects are usually enlisted by luxury brands for the design of their corporate buildings, museums and retail spaces, but they have often engaged with smaller products as well: in 2021 alone, Rem Koolhaas' firm OMA revisited the exclusive American Express Centurion credit card (Barba, 2021); Frank Gehry, who designed the Fondation Louis Vuitton, created the bottle for the Maison's Les Extraits fragrance line (Kim, 2021); Kengo Kuma partnered with Portuguese eyewear VAVA for two 3D-printed glasses' styles (Hawkins, 2021).

In their effort to provoke the audience with unconventional art crossovers, luxury brands have also looked beyond the traditional *holy trinity of Vasari* – architecture, sculpture and painting – to engage with other artistic disciplines, such as the performing arts: Dom Pérignon has worked on the design of limited-edition bottles with Hollywood filmmaker David Lynch and, most recently, with pop singer and actress Lady Gaga (Terrill, 2012; Dom Pérignon, 2022). In 2018, beauty brand Aesop commissioned Oscar-winning film director and screenwriter Luca Guadagnino with the interior design of their signature store in Rome (Levy, 2018); in the same year, niche perfumery brand D.S. & Durga involved pop rock band Duran Duran to sign a line of four fragrances (Duran Duran, 2018). In his time as music mogul, Pharrell Williams engaged in a plurality of collaborative projects for Chanel: in 2014, Pharrell featured in the late Karl Lagerfeld's short movie *Reincarnation*, for which he also composed the main track (Socha, 2014); five years later, he co-designed a street-art-inspired capsule collection (Ingvaldsen, 2019). To launch its White Caviar beauty line, Swiss skincare brand La Prairie commissioned Taiwanese choreographer Wen-Chi Su with the dance piece *Moving Towards the Horizon*, which was exclusively presented during Art Basel Miami Beach 2021 (Fontaine, 2021).

In some cases, the expressive charge of a collaborative project is released through the dissonance between the glamorous aura traditionally emanating from luxury brands and the irreverent style of an artist. Such is the instance of fine spirit house Hennessy, which has pushed its artistic collaborations to the limits with underground artmakers such as Shepard Fairey and Futura (Hofmann, 2015).

Market data confirms consumers' penchant for inventiveness in luxury brand and art collaborations: according to the 2021 *New Luxury Survey* by Highsnobiety, 85 per cent of the respondents "enjoy when traditional brands go in unexpected creative directions", and two-thirds appreciate brands that implement a great collaboration programme (Lamas, 2021). In order to increase their spectacular appeal and lead their audiences to "fresh and exciting heights" (Bulaong, 2021), luxury brand and art collaborations are evolving into ensemble programmes, which unfold across various artistic initiatives, products and media content.

For the Ruinart commission in 2018, the Chinese camouflage artist Liu Bolin produced a series of chameleon-like portraits of the Maison's employees and himself, documenting his work in a making-of video. The photographs were exhibited in 30 art fairs, among which were included Art Basel, Frieze and the International Contemporary Art Fair (FIAC). During the project's launch event, Bolin performed his *disappearance* in a reproduction of *The Oyster Dinner* (1735) by Jean-François de Troy, which is believed to be the first painting in history to portray a bottle of champagne (Serafin, 2019). Bolin then repurposed the jackets he wore during his project to decorate ten numbered, Ruinart Blanc de Blancs jeroboam boxes (LVMH, 2018).

Latest developments in the NFT technology have further amplified the reach and the richness of these collaborative ensembles. In 2021, Glenfiddich launched the Grande Composition and invited 17 artists worldwide to reimagine the brand's filigree motif for the box of its latest single malt whisky Grande Couronne. Digital artist Stephanie Fung was then commissioned to create crypto-fashion pieces inspired by three of the Grande Composition artworks, which were subsequently auctioned as NFTs (Bulaong, 2021).

Similarly, Pernod Ricard's whisky brand Royal Salute has collaborated with British fashion designer Richard Quinn on one of their Pinnacle Blends, The House of Quinn. The 200-hand-blown, black crystal decanters have been decorated with Quinn's petal and thorn motif, detailed in gold leaf. The motif is also reproduced on a silk pocket square, part of the ensemble. Furthermore, the first bottle of the limited edition has been accompanied by one-of-one NFT, which was put on sale through specialised marketplace BlockBar (Royal Salute, 2021).

Rather than just releasing a single hybrid product, these programmes create an extravaganza of "image-objects" (Debord, 1994, p. 10), i.e., tangible products and digital by-products, video contents and events that are accessed through a plurality of platforms and formats, from the YouTube video to the NFTs bid.

The eclectic manipulation of fragments

Juxtapositions originate from, and thrive on, fragments. As discussed above, postmodernity shatters the monolithic solidity of clear-cut categories, consistent narratives and defined aesthetics, scattering around a concoction of material, conceptual and visual debris.

The recent Covid-19 pandemic has prompted luxury brands to further reflect on the theme of fragmentation through their art collaborations. In 2020, Prada split the digital fashion show of its Spring/Summer 2021 collection into five short movies directed by five contemporary artists across a range of different disciplines, from filmmaking to photography (Claudel, 2020). According to head designer Miuccia Prada, both the collection – aptly titled Multiple Views – and the format of the show were meant to artistically echo the sense of fracture underpinning our present reality: "the world today is so complicated, so full of different peoples, countries, religions. You cannot have a unitary vision" (Prada, in Zargani, 2020). In the same year, Loewe's creative director Jonathan Anderson chose to present the men's and womenswear collections through an array of items – a paintbrush, a vinyl record, paper looks, a T-shirt, a music sheet, etc. – which were boxed and sent via post to the fashion show audience. Through the engagement with those miscellaneous items, the remote audience was thus left to piece together the concept behind the collections (Yotka, 2020a; Yotka, 2020b). Anderson continued his reflection on fragmentation in the Fall/Winter 2021 menswear and women's pre-collection, where he referenced the assemblage art of Joe Brainard with looks inspired by the artists' collage works, sketches and pansy flowers. This time Anderson presented a Show in a Book: the audience received at home a volume on Brainard containing in the pockets of its dusk jacket the booklets of the two collections (Jana, 2021). The influence of Brainard on Anderson, however, is not limited to fashion design. In Anderson's view, Brainard's artistic collages express the composite nature of Loewe's brand universe, which is composed of a mosaic of tangible and intangible outputs – four fashion lines, the Loewe Foundation and its Craft Prize (Jana, 2021).

In being picked up and assembled into hybrid objects, cross-disciplinary codes and eclectic meanings, fragments are severed from their primary context. Nonetheless, they still retain traces of their origins, which luxury brand and art collaborations often leverage to enthuse the audience with evocative references to other dimensions or atmospherics.

One case in point is the Louis Vuitton's Masters handbag collection, designed by art star Jeff Koons in 2017. For this collaboration Koons revisited his *Gazing Ball* paintings series of 2015, where he placed blue mirrored glass balls on large-scale copies of Old Masters and modern paintings – from Titian's *The Pastoral Concert* (c.1509) to Édouard Manet's *The Luncheon on the Grass* (1863). Similarly, in the Masters' collaboration masterpieces of

Western art are printed onto the silhouettes of Louis Vuitton's iconic bags, with the painter's name written in gold or silver metallic letters at the centre and the monograms of Jeff Koons and Louis Vuitton appearing at the corners (Les Façons, 2017). Each Masters bag features inside the biography of the painter whose work is reproduced on the canvas; hanging outside is a leather rabbit bag charm, nodding to Koons' celebrated *Rabbit* sculptural trio of 1986 (Koons, 2017).

The collaborative project with Louis Vuitton carries forward Koons' exploration of art appropriation as a way to establish a "dialogue" (Koons, 2017) with artists across time. Already in 2013, Koons had designed the Balloon Venus box for the Dom Pérignon Rosé Vintage 2003 as a miniature version of his eight-feet-high, stainless-steel sculpture *Venus*, which in turn is a Neo-kitsch reinterpretation of the Upper Paleolithic *Venus of Willendorf* (Lynch, 2013; Sotheby's, 2020a). The *Gazing Ball* paintings series is in itself a reiteration of Koons' *Gazing Ball* project of 2013, where the blue reflective spheres had been affixed to replicas of classical sculptures (Lansroth, 2015).

Through his work with the gazing balls, Koons intends to further deepen our connection with art: by allowing the viewers to see their image reflected inside iconic artworks of the past, the gazing balls offer them the opportunity to "time-travel" (Koons, 2017) in the world of the masterpiece. In the Louis Vuitton Masters bags, however, the volumetric reflective power of the gazing balls is flattened and constricted into the bi-dimensional shiny letters composing the Old Masters' names and the initials of Louis Vuitton and Jeff Koons. As a matter of fact, the owners and the viewers of the handbags are denied the possibility to become an integral part of history: rather, they are left to grasp only suggestions of it through the printed paintings replacing the traditional monogrammed canvas, the evocative aura exuding from a "Da Vinci" or a "Van Gogh" name and a few paragraphs of information about the artist inside the bag.

In reviewing the first Gazing Ball series, critics emphasised the empty, almost ghostly nature of Koons' sculptural replicas, which ends up conjuring the absence of the originals instead of bringing them back to life (Gingeras, 2013). In the Louis Vuitton Masters collection, the past gets somehow disarticulated and dispersed across different elements – the replica of the paintings, the metallic letters, the master's biography, the rabbit charm. These fragments are not able to recompose the *fil rouge* connecting centuries of art making; nonetheless, they are able to stimulate a sensorial and symbolic interaction with the handbag and, through the handbag, with art. The same Koons seems to be ultimately leaning towards a spectacularised appreciation of art history based on fragmented yet impactful stimuli, rather than on the nuanced and comprehensive understanding of the masterpieces within their own context: "they are very iconic works – but you don't need to know anything, it's just about the reaction to something. It's about you, it's about the viewer, how you feel" (Koons, in Ellison, 2017; Armitage, 2020).

Above and beyond: Hyperreality and its enhanced atmospherics

Postmodern consumption does not settle on the hopeful longing for unity and context, but it feeds off a sense of liberated recreation: spectacular juxtapositions and the playful manipulation of fragments release both producers and consumers from following any pre-existing exegesis and empower them to allocate sensational meanings to products and experiences (Holt, 2002; Appadurai, 2005; Baudrillard, 2017). This aesthetic resignification of consumption ultimately ends up transfiguring reality into a symbolic world, an apparent hyperreality populated by physical and content objects with no distinction "between the real and the simulation, the material and the imaginary, the product and the image" (Firat and Venkatesh, 1995, p. 250).

By releasing a plurality of tangible products, digital assets, contents and events, luxury brand and art collaborations generate their own hyperreality. Let us consider a few examples.

In 2021, London's Design Museum hosted the exhibition *Charlotte Perriand: The Modern Life* – iteration of the one organised a couple of years earlier at Fondation Louis Vuitton to commemorate the work of the French designer and architect. For the occasion, displayed in the central atrium of the Design Museum was *Rémy Martin: The Centaur*, a mobile sculpture by Charles Kaisin consisting of 1724 centaurs hand-gilded by family-run craft studio Atelier Thiery. The sculpture meant to reference sponsor LVMH's cognac brand Rémy Martin by reinterpreting its centaur logo and foundation date (1724) and celebrating at the same time French craftsmanship as shared legacy among Perriand, Rémy Martin and Atelier Thiery. Atelier Thiery also designed a limited-edition bottle for the Rémy Martin XO cognac, which was released for exclusive purchase at Selfridges (Keays, 2021).

For its collaboration with adidas in 2020, 300-year-old and counting porcelain maker Meissen customised the ZX8000 sneaker with a hand-painted collage of 15 among their iconic patterns with ceramic overlays. The Porcelain sneaker was then auctioned at Sotheby's and the sale proceeds donated to the Brooklyn Museum to support youth art programmes (Sotheby's, 2020b). Fashion designer Paul Smith joined the 2018 edition of the Secret 7" charity project, where 700 creatives are yearly invited to anonymously design a record sleeve for a selected well-known track. The 700-piece sleeves collection is displayed in an exhibition before the records being blind-sold on a first-come-first-served basis (Hitti, 2018). With the aim to bring its travel history into the metaverse, Rimowa teamed with multidisciplinary design company NUOVA to create four NFTs artworks themed around the German maker's workmanship: the series, named Blueprints from the Metaverse, was auctioned in 2021 on NFTs marketplace Rarible, with proceeds donated to NUOVA and to an unnamed non-profit humanitarian organisation (Kelly, 2021).

The instances above highlight how the consumption of these collaborative outputs goes well beyond the purchase of a specific product: very few buyers could actually get hold of a bottle of Rémy Martin XO or a Secret 7" vinyl, even a smaller number of NFT collectors was able to access the digital art pieces of Rimowa X NUOVA, and only one winning bidder acquired the adidas X Meissen sneaker. Visiting the Perriand or the Secret 7" shows, as well as bidding on Sotheby's or Rarible, captures only one facet of the collaborations. With the increasing complexity of the collaborative projects in terms of outputs, formats and platforms, their full appreciation increasingly happens at a symbolic level and only through articles, images, press releases or any other media content on newspapers and websites. In other words, marketing storytelling becomes the *glutinum mundi* (glue of the world), i.e., the element holding together the hyperreal world of luxury brand and art collaborations.

Unfolding across reality and fantasy, hyper reality is by definition an enhanced dimension. Two recent short films produced by luxury brands and featuring performance artists play with details from different epochs to recreate an atmospheric richer than reality.

Reincarnation (2014), directed by Karl Lagerfeld and featuring Pharrell Williams, Cara Delevingne and Geraldine Chaplin, was meant to retrace the origins of the iconic Chanel jacket's design, which was allegedly inspired by the uniform of a lift attendant in a hotel close to Salzburg in the 1950s (Chanel, 2014). The movie storyline, however, is a far cry from a historical account. The encounter between Coco Chanel (Chaplin) and the lift boy (Pharrell) in the Salzburg hotel overlaps and intertwines with other historical interpositions: hanging in the hotel hall, the portraits of emperor Franz Joseph I and empress Elisabeth of Austria recall the illustrious Austro-Hungarian empire of the second half of 19th century. While the portraits reproduce the iconic appearances of the imperial couple as immortalised at the time by royal portrait painter Franz Xaver Winterhalter, a close-up reveals another temporal twist: the facial traits of Franz Joseph and Elisabeth are actually those of contemporary stars Pharrell Williams and Cara Delevingne. Bringing simultaneously alive the atmospheres of the 19th, 20th and 21st centuries, Pharrell/ Franz and Cara/Elisabeth jump out of their portraits and sing and dance in the hotel's hall at the rhythm of Pharrell's soundtrack *CC The World*.

A similar temporal syncretism characterises Tiffany's 2021 campaign "About Love" (Spellings, 2021; Tiffany & Co., 2021). The short movie features singer and songwriter Beyoncé wearing the Tiffany Yellow Diamond and singing *Moon River* at the piano, while husband and producer Jay-Z films her. In the background is the painting *Equals Pi* (1982) by Jean-Michel Basquiat, whose main colour theme visually recalls Tiffany's trademarked robin egg blue. The one-minute-and-a-half-long film is a kaleidoscope of allusions: the song *Moon River* refers back to *Breakfast at Tiffany's*, the 1961 movie adaptation of Truman Capote's eponymous novel starring actress

Audrey Hepburn. Hepburn herself wore the Tiffany Yellow Diamond for the movie's promotional shooting; most recently, the Diamond made the headlines again appearing on Lady Gaga at the 2019 Academy Awards. In order to further enrich the collaborative project with another historical legacy, Tiffany's executive Vice President Alexandre Arnault even suggested that Basquiat's colour choice in *Equals Pi* was an intentional reference to Tiffany's, although the claim has been dismissed by art experts for lack of evidence (Friedman, 2021).

While there is certainly legitimacy in the scholarly debate about *Equals Pi* and its links to Tiffany's, it should be noted that authenticity is not the validating principle of a hyperreality: as a matter of fact, by blending facts and fantasies to titillate consumers' senses and imagination, hyperreality bends historical and factual accuracy in favour of glossed suggestions to it. This, however, does not disprove authenticity altogether; it just shifts its referent: in a hyperreal environment "authenticity is not intrinsic to the object, but rather related to subjective feeling and experience as well as contexts" (Bai, 2018, p. 217). Gucci's former creative director Alessandro Michele artistically reflected on the concept of authenticity with art provocateur Maurizio Cattelan in 2018, when they organised an exhibition of reproductions and replicas at the Yuz Museum in Shanghai – the title of the exhibition itself is a citation of Marina Abramović's performance retrospective at MoMA in 2010: *The Artist is Present* (Choy, 2018). Similar to Koons' idea of art appropriation as a dialogue between artists, Michele stresses the creative process underpinning the assemblage of fragments or the use of copies in opposition to the passive act of copying: "one creates a conversation and isn't really copying. It would be like saying Mozart copied his compositions because he used musical notes. […] I don't replicate something in my work because I need the replica. I do it because I need the note" (Michele, in Haramis, 2018). From this perspective, the Yellow Diamond or the portraits of the Austrian imperial couple are all notes used to compose richer sensorial symphonies: in the hyperreal world of luxury brand and art collaborations, it is not authenticity, but the spectacular appeal of authenticity, that ultimately matters.

CASE

Peculiar Contrast, Perfect Light: Virgil Abloh's extravagant display

> it's not just fashion or films we make, it's space for new stories and artworks to be placed
>
> (Virgil Abloh, 2021)

For the Louis Vuitton Fall/Winter 2021 menswear collection, late creative director Virgil Abloh explored the theme of black condition. Abloh dubbed the collection Ebonics, a term that acknowledges African-American English as its own language rather than just a spoiled version of the conventional American. Ebonics was presented as a short film titled *Peculiar Contrast, Perfect Light* and streamed on the Maison's YouTube channel at the virtual Paris Fashion Week (Natividad, 2021).

The show opens with a reference to the essay "Stranger in the Village" (1953) by James Baldwin, an account of the novelist's sense of alienation as a black man living across Switzerland and USA: slam-poet and singer Saul Williams walks across a snowy alpine landscape with a Louis Vuitton monogrammed silver briefcase in his hands. Williams then enters a lobby-like closed space and continues walking among passing-by models, reciting an invitation to repair black discrimination in the name of prominent figures from all times and places – from Walt Whitman to Gandhi, from Steve Biko to Rumi, from Obatala to Federico Fellini (Louis Vuitton, 2021).

In concluding his spell-like recitation, Williams puts down his briefcase. This marks the beginning of another artistic moment: the camera shifts to a dancer performing among still models, while gender poet and activist Kai-Isaiah Jamal accompanies the dance with lyrics calling marginalised groups to take the world, as the world "takes so much from us" (Jamal, in Natividad, 2021). As a symbolic baton, the Louis Vuitton briefcase is then passed on to musician Yasiin Bey (Mos Def), whose rap performance accompanies models walking down the catwalk and disappearing into a luminous background (Louis Vuitton, 2021).

Peculiar Contrast, Perfect Light fully articulates the postmodern dimensions explored so far. Firstly, it dramatises blackness in the aftermath of Black Lives Matter: in their fight to deconstruct the racial archetypes and biases of modernity, black people are negotiating their existence between displacement and sense of belonging. This contradictory yet so postmodern condition finds echo in the hybrid and inconclusive format of the show. *Peculiar Contrast, Perfect Light* dismisses any definitive affiliation to one disciplinary category: as loosely described by Abloh (2021) in the quote above, it is not just "fashion", it is not just a "film". Rather, the show is conceived as a "multidisciplinary artistic expression of ideas investigated within the collection" (show notes, in Robinson, 2021).

The suggestive juxtapositions of different art forms in *Peculiar Contrast, Perfect Light* also stimulate the audience's interest. One of the discussion threads in the YouTube comment section considers the inspiration behind the modernist set of the show. For its green marble walls and white Barcelona chairs, video-watcher Kazuma8630 (2021) points out the set's stylistic and materialistic resemblance to the Barcelona Pavilion (1929) by architect Ludwig Mies van der Rohe and interior designer Lilly Reich. While many appreciate the added value of background knowledge in art and architecture for "it adds a different level of appreciation" (Ambreen, 2021), others direct their appreciation to the transformative work of Virgil Abloh on these references: "I thought the reference was more his collages than the Barcelona pavilion itself" (Fatmé Condé, 2021).

The resulting hyperreal atmosphere of *Peculiar Contrast, Perfect Light*, with intertwining material and content features from performative arts, design, architecture and fashion, ultimately activates a sensorial response from the audience: "the music and the fashion, the diversity, the art. I was emotional watching it" (Loveandthings479, 2021).

Considerations

As mentioned in the introduction, the contemporary evolutions in the engagement of luxury brands with the arts have been conventionally framed within a luxury strategy for companies to regain that aura of uniqueness and rarity that the adoption of a capitalistic mode of production has tarnished. *Peculiar Contrast, Perfect Light*, as well as other recent collaborative instances, shows that in their approach to art collaborations luxury brands have widened their views beyond the spillover effect of art's aesthetic qualities onto their products (Hagtvedt and Patrick, 2008) and consider the context of postmodern marketplace, where the commercial and the aesthetic feed off each other. In an aestheticised consumption scenario shaped around the quest for enriched and sensorially augmented products, the value of collaborations ultimately stems from the spectacular elevation that luxury brands are able to generate around their outputs.

Virgil Abloh treated the show as a creative space, where he assembled and recomposed semantic and sensorial elements drawn from music, dance, poetry, literature, architecture, fashion. In addition, like a nested doll, Abloh inserted *Peculiar Contrast, Perfect Light* as part of a wider series of digital and physical collaborative initiatives during the Paris Fashion Week, collectively named "Louis Vuitton: a Walk in the Park" and consisting of a pop-up space in Rue Pont Neuf decorated with art pieces by skateboarder Lucien Clarke and the custom-made skate park/art installation by Galerie Kreo (Robinson, 2021). In this way, Abloh was able to create a Louis Vuitton hyperreal world in Paris, where the presentation of the new collection was linked to the Spring/Summer collection, available for purchase at the pop-up store, and to the glamorised skate culture of Clarke and Galerie Kreo. This meant for Louis Vuitton to reach multiple clusters of different consumers: from the YouTube watcher to the fashion customer, from the Paris Fashion Week audience to the fandom of the artists featured in those collaborative initiatives.

Similar to Jeff Koons or Alessandro Michele, Abloh reflected on the issues of appropriation (Bettridge, 2018; Delistraty, 2018) pointing out that originality does not lie in the object, but on the emotions that his assemblages are able to elicit in the viewers: "using my vocabulary can get a different emotion out of something that you've already seen" (Chan, 2017). Through *Peculiar Contrast, Perfect Light*, Abloh further demonstrates that it is the ability to masterfully play with references and suggestions from a variety of sources, and to combine them into a rich network of themes, formats and touchpoints, that eventually delivers the spectacle value of the outputs.

Note

1 As a historical category, postmodernity refers to the Western post-industrial society of the late 19th century and its subsequent evolutions into the information society in the late 20th century. Although its tenets, leading figures and watershed moments greatly differ depending on the area considered – arts, literature, science and knowledge, politics, economics (Lyotard, 1984; Jameson, 1991; Anderson, 1998) – in general terms postmodernity is defined as "a social condition, a climate of opinion, or a cultural mood" (Delanty, 2000, p. 142) distinct from the paradigms and assumptions of modernity. Scholars have been discussing whether the relationship between modernity and postmodernity should be framed in terms of continuity or fracture, as many aspects of postmodernity were already present in earlier periods (Featherstone, 2007). A few have downplayed the issue altogether, posing that both modernity and postmodernity are ultimately artificial constructs of our times (Bauman, 1992; Anderson, 1998). Here, postmodernity is considered a cluster of cultural traits – both inherent and originating from the modern period – that have coalesced into a worldview, thus orienting the perspectives of current societies towards the world and its phenomena.

Bibliography

Abloh, V. (2021) *usually I have run-on-sentences for days but today I don't. my whole being has been poured out into this film here*, 21 January [Instagram]. Available at: https://www.instagram.com/p/CKT5YQYphtM/ (Accessed: 14 April 2022).

Ambreen, S. (2021) *Glad I learnt that in class just before seeing the live* [YouTube]. Available at: https://www.youtube.com/watch?v=vV_QoQD_nrA (Accessed: 25 April 2022).

Anderson, P. (1998) *The Origins of Postmodernity*. London: Verso Books.

Appadurai, A. (2005) *Modernity at Large: Cultural Dimensions of Globalization*. Minneapolis: University of Minnesota Press.

Armitage, J. (2020) *Luxury and Visual Culture*. London: Bloomsbury.

Bai, Y. (2018) "Artification and authenticity: museum exhibitions of luxury fashion brands in China", in A. Vänskä and H. Clark (eds.) *Fashion Curating: Critical Practice in the Museum and Beyond*. London: Bloomsbury Academic, pp. 213–228.

Barba, J.J. (2021) "OMA designs the exclusive Amex credit card, with Boompjes original drawings", *Metalocus*, 15 August. Available at: https://www.metalocus.es/en/news/oma-designs-exclusive-amex-credit-card-boompjes-original-drawings (Accessed: 27 February 2022).

Bardhi, F. and Eckhardt, G.M. (2017) "Liquid consumption", *Journal of Consumer Research*, 44/3, pp. 582–597. Available at: https://doi.org/10.1093/jcr/ucx050.

Baudrillard, J. (2017) *The Consumer Society: Myths and Structures*. London: Sage Publications.

Bauman, Z. (1992) *Intimations of Postmodernity*. London: Routledge.

Bauman, Z. (1995) *Life in Fragments: Essays in Postmodern Morality*. Oxford: Blackwell Publishing.

Bauman, Z. (1997) *Postmodernity and Its Discontents*. Cambridge: Polity Press.

Bauman, Z. (2000) *Liquid Modernity*. Cambridge: Polity Press.

Benjamin, W. (1999) *The Arcades Project*. Translated by H. Eiland and K. McLaughlin. Cambridge: The Belknap Press of Harvard University Press.

Bettridge, T. (2018) "Virgil Abloh: 'Duchamp is my lawyer'", *032c*, 26 March. Available at: https://032c.com/magazine/duchamp-is-my-lawyer-virgil-abloh (Accessed: 1 May 2022).

Boltanski, L. and Esquerre, A. (2020) *Enrichment: A Critique of Commodities*. Translated by C. Porter. Cambridge: Polity Press.

Bruhn, C. (2016) "On guard: ROOM by Antony Gormley", *ArchitectureAU*, 23 November. Available at: https://architectureau.com/articles/room-by-anthony-gormley/ (Accessed: 27 February 2022).

Bulaong, M. (2021) "Glenfiddich explores crypto fashion and art to celebrate cultural mavericks", *Highsnobiety*, no date. Available at: https://www.highsnobiety.com/p/glenfiddich-crypto-fashion/ (Accessed: 27 February 2022).

Chan, S. (2017) "Virgil Abloh on collaborating with Ikea, designing emotion into objects", *The Hollywood Reporter*, 9 October. Available at: https://www.hollywoodreporter.com/lifestyle/style/virgil-abloh-talks-ikea-collaboration-1046889/ (Accessed: 1 May 2022).

Chanel (2014) *"Reincarnation" film by Karl Lagerfeld ft. P. Williams, C. Delevingne & G. Chaplin*, 1 December [YouTube]. Available at: https://www.youtube.com/watch?v=wO4-TV6Zckc (Accessed: 6 March 2022).

Choy, Y. (2018) "Gucci and Maurizio Cattelan explore the power of appropriation in Shanghai show", *Wallpaper*, 19 October. Available at: https://www.wallpaper.com/fashion/gucci-maurizio-cattelan-the-artist-is-present-shanghai (Accessed: 7 April 2022).

Claudel, M. (2020) "Prada presents Multiple Views: a collection of 5 films directed by leading contemporary artists", *Vogue France*, 15 July. Available at: https://www.vogue.fr/fashion/article/prada-multiple-views-collection-artists-digital (Accessed: 6 March 2022).

Debord, G. (1994) *Society of the Spectacle*. Translated by K. Knabb. London: Rebel Press.

Delanty, G. (2000) *Modernity and Postmodernity: Knowledge, Power and the Self*. London: Sage Publications.

Delistraty, C. (2018) "The endless appropriations of Virgil Abloh", *Garage*, 21 January. Available at: https://garage.vice.com/en_us/article/paq4p7/appropriations-virgil-abloh (Accessed: 1 May 2022).

Dom Pérignon (2022) *Lady Gaga and Dom Pérignon*. Available at: https://www.domperignon.com/uk-en/inspirations/lady-gaga (Accessed: 3 March 2022).

Duran Duran (2018) *Duran Duran Collaborate with D.S. & Durga on Limited Edition Fragrance Collection*, 8 October. Available at: https://duranduran.com/2018/duran-duran-collaborate-with-d-s-durga-on-limited-edition-fragrance-collection/ (Accessed: 3 March 2022).

Ellison, J. (2017) "Master pieces? Jeff Koons on his first collaboration with Louis Vuitton", *Financial Times*, 11 April. Available at: https://www.ft.com/content/354c71d0-1dfe-11e7-b7d3-163f5a7f229c (Accessed: 10 March 2022).

Fatmé Condé (2021) *I thought the reference was more his collages* [YouTube]. Available at: https://www.youtube.com/watch?v=vV_QoQD_nrA (Accessed: 25 April 2022).

Featherstone, M. (2007) *Consumer Culture and Postmodernism*. London: Sage Publications.

Firat, A.F. and Venkatesh, A. (1995) "Liberatory postmodernism and the reenchantment of consumption", *Journal of Consumer Research*, 22/3, pp. 239–267. Available at: https://doi.org/10.1086/209448.

Fontaine, P. (2021) "Wen-Chi Su captures the dance of light and water for La Prairie", *Whitewall*, 24 November. Available at: https://whitewall.art/lifestyle/wen-chi-su-captures-the-dance-of-light-and-water-for-la-prairie (Accessed: 27 February 2022).

Friedman, V. (2021) "The mystery of that Basquiat painting – and its Tiffany blue", *The New York Times*, 4 September. Available at: https://www.nytimes.com/2021/09/01/style/tiffany-basquiat-jay-z-beyonce.html (Accessed: 6 March 2022).

Gingeras, A.M. (2013) "Instant Classic'", *Artforum International*, 52/1, pp. 145–146.

Hagtvedt, H. and Patrick, V.M. (2008) "Art infusion: the influence of visual art on the perception and evaluation of consumer products", *Journal of Marketing Research*, 45/3, pp. 379–389. Available at: https://doi.org/10.1509/jmkr.45.3.379.

Haramis, N. (2018) "Gucci's Alessandro Michele on authenticity in the age of artifice", *Interview*, 11 December. Available at: https://www.interviewmagazine.com/culture/alessandro-michele-gucci-on-authenticity-in-the-age-of-artifice (Accessed: 24 March 2021).

Hawkins, L. (2021) "Kengo Kuma sunglasses: wearable architecture?", *Wallpaper*, 19 June. Available at: https://www.wallpaper.com/fashion/kengo-kuma-sunglasses-vava-collaboration (Accessed: 27 February 2022).

Hitti, N. (2018) "Anish Kapoor and Es Devlin create secret designs for charity vinyl sleeves", *Dezeen*, 4 May. Available at: https://www.dezeen.com/2018/05/04/secret-7-record-vinyl-sleeves-anish-kapoor-es-devlin-jean-jullien/ (Accessed: 24 March 2022).

Hofmann, R. (2015) "Strange bedfellows: the new mashup of big booze and street art", *Punch*, 29 September. Available at: https://punchdrink.com/articles/the-new-mashup-of-spirits-brands-and-artists-1800-tequila-keith-haring-absolut-warhol/ (Accessed: 27 February 2022).

Holt, D.B. (2002) "Why do brands cause trouble? A dialectical theory of consumer culture and branding", *Journal of Consumer Research*, 29/1, pp. 70–90. Available at: https://doi.org/10.1086/339922.

Hughes, G. (2003) *Transcendence and History: The Search for Ultimacy from Ancient Societies to Postmodernity*. Columbia: University of Missouri Press.

Ingvaldsen, T. (2019) "Inside the 'Chanel Pharrell' capsule release at the luxury house's Seoul flagship", *Hypebeast*, 29 March. Available at: https://hypebeast.com/2019/3/chanel-pharrell-spring-summer-2019-collection-seoul-store-release (Accessed: 4 March 2022).

Jameson, F. (1991) *Postmodernism, or, the Cultural Logic of Late Capitalism*. London: Verso Books.

Jana, R. (2021) "Peek inside Loewe's 'Show in a Book' with Jonathan Anderson", *Vogue*, 22 January. Available at: https://www.vogue.com/article/loewe-show-in-a-book-mens-fall-2021 (Accessed: 21 June 2021).

Kazuma8630 (2021) *For all the people, who don't study architecture* [YouTube]. Available at: https://www.youtube.com/watch?v=vV_QoQD_nrA (Accessed: 25 April 2022).

Keays, M. (2021) "Rémy Martin's mobile sculpture at Design Museum London", *Wallpaper*, 17 June. Available at: https://www.wallpaper.com/design/remy-martin-mobile-sculpture-design-museum-london (Accessed: 24 March 2022).

Kelly, D. (2021) "Rimowa enters the metaverse with first-ever NFTs collection", *Hypebeast*, 11 May. Available at: https://hypebeast.com/2021/5/rimowa-nft-collection-metaverse-auction-new-release-info (Accessed: 4 April 2022).

Kim, Y.E. (2021) "Frank Gehry designs Louis Vuitton's latest perfume bottles", *Hypebae*, 8 July. Available at: https://hypebae.com/2021/7/louis-vuitton-perfumes-les-extraits-collection-frank-gehry-bottle-design-collaboration-rhapsody-symphony (Accessed: 27 February 2022).

Koons, J. (2017) "The history of art according to Jeff Koons", *Harper's Bazaar*, 12 October. Available at: https://www.harpersbazaar.com/culture/art-books-music/a12823707/jeff-koons-art-history/ (Accessed: 7 March 2022).

Lamas, T. (2021) "Collabs are the new relationships", *Data Breach*, 17 June [Highsnobiety monthly newsletter].

Lansroth, B. (2015) 'Jeff Koons exhibition at the Gagosian Gallery presents Gazing Balls – a showcase of the artist's three-dimensional objects conjured on canvas', *Widewalls*, 18 November. Available at: https://www.widewalls.ch/magazine/jeff-koons-exhibition-gazing-ball (Visited: 10 OctOber 2023).

Les Façons (2017) *Louis Vuitton Masters Collection by Jeff Koons*, 12 April [YouTube]. Available at: https://www.youtube.com/watch?v=kvbNJ4UXZHc (Accessed: 6 October 2023).

Levy, N. (2018) "Aesop teams up with film director Luca Guadagnino for interior of Rome store", *Dezeen*, 22 October. Available at: https://www.dezeen.com/2018/10/22/aesop-store-film-director-luca-guadagnino-rome-interiors/ (Accessed: 4 March 2022).

Louis Vuitton (2021) *Men's Fall-Winter 2021 Fashion Show*, 21 January [YouTube]. Available at: https://www.youtube.com/watch?v=vV_QoQD_nrA (Accessed: 21 March 2022).

Loveandthings479 (2021) *Omg as soon as mos def starts rapping you're trapped* [YouTube]. Available at: https://www.youtube.com/watch?v=vV_QoQD_nrA (Accessed: 25 April 2022).

LVMH (2018) *Ruinart Presents Collaboration with Artist Liu Bolin*, 16 March. Available at: https://www.lvmh.com/news-documents/news/ruinart-presents-collaboration-with-artist-liu-bolin/ (Accessed: 27 February 2022).

LVMH (2019) *Louis Vuitton Artycapucines Collection Invites Six Artists to Revisit the Iconic Capucines bag*, 7 June. Available at: https://www.lvmh.com/news-documents/news/louis-vuitton-artycapucines-collection-invites-six-artists-to-revisit-the-iconic-capucines-bag/ (Accessed: 27 February 2022).

Lynch, M. (2013) "Pop bottles: Jeff Koons teams with Dom Pérignon", *WWD*, 27 June. Available at: https://wwd.com/fashion-news/designer-luxury/pop-bottles-jeff-koons-teams-with-dom-prignon-7025031/ (Accessed: 7 March 2022).

Lyotard, J.F. (1984) *The Postmodern Condition: A Report on Knowledge*. Translated by G. Bennington and B. Massumi. Minneapolis: University of Minnesota Press.

Natividad, A. (2021) "Louis Vuitton casts otherness as power in hypno[t]ic new film", *Muse by Clio*, 1 February. Available at: https://musebycl.io/fashion-beauty/louis-vuitton-casts-otherness-power-hypnonic-new-film (Accessed: 14 April 2022).

Pillay, N. (2021) "Veuve Clicquot taps Yayoi Kusama to dress up its new vintage champagne, La Grande Dame 2012", *Harper's Bazaar Singapore*, 23 November. Available at: https://www.harpersbazaar.com.sg/life/veuve-clicquot-taps-yayoi-kusama-to-dress-up-its-new-vintage-champagne-la-grande-dame-2012/ (Accessed: 27 February 2022).

Portee, A. (2021) "Dior unveils twelve artists' Dior Lady Art handbags for their sixth edition", *Forbes*, 21 December. Available at: https://www.forbes.com/sites/allysonportee/2021/12/21/dior-unveils-twelve-artists-dior-lady-art-handbags-for-their-sixth-edition/?sh=164f67fe2ef7 (Accessed: 27 February 2022).

Robinson, R. (2021) "Virgil Abloh's Louis Vuitton concept store boosts digital only Men's Paris Fashion Week", *Forbes*, 22 January. Available at: https://www.forbes.com/sites/roxannerobinson/2021/01/22/virgil-ablohs-louis-vuitton-concept-store-boosts-digital-only-mens-paris-fashion-week/ (Accessed: 21 March 2022).

Rolls-Royce (2022) *Phantom Gallery*. Available at: https://www.rolls-roycemotorcars.com/en_US/inspiring-greatness/objects/phantom-gallery.html (Accessed: 27 February 2022).

Rolls-Royce Motor Cars Pressclub (2020) *Celebrated artist Dr. Esther Mahlangu paints unique artwork for Rolls-Royce Phantom Gallery*, 13 February. Available at: https://www.press.rolls-roycemotorcars.com/rolls-royce-motor-cars-pressclub/article/detail/T0305553EN/celebrated-artist-dr-esther-mahlangu-paints-unique-artwork-for-rolls-royce-phantom-gallery?language=en (Accessed: 27 February 2022).

Rolls-Royce Motor Cars Pressclub (2022) *Phantom Orchid an inspirational symbol for our times*, 27 January. Available at: https://www.press.rolls-roycemotorcars.com/rolls-royce-motor-cars-pressclub/article/detail/T0365954EN/phantom-orchid-an-inspirational-symbol-for-our-times (Accessed: 27 February 2022).

Royal Salute (2021) *The House of Quinn by Richard Quinn*. Available at: https://www.royalsalute.com/en/whisky/the-house-of-quinn-by-richard-quinn/ (Accessed: 27 February 2022).

Segran, E. (2018) "Olafur Eliasson's clever trick for coping with hellacious travel", *Fast Company*, 27 November. Available at: https://www.fastcompany.com/90272399/olafur-eliassons-clever-trick-for-coping-with-hellacious-travel (Accessed: 27 February 2022).

Serafin, A. (2019) "Artist Liu Bolin explores the hidden depths of champagne production at French house Ruinart", *Wallpaper*, 3 January. Available at: https://www.wallpaper.com/design/liu-bolin-ruinart-champagne-production (Accessed: 27 February 2022).

Socha, M. (2014) "Pharrell Williams and Karl Lagerfeld in collaboration", *WWD*, 22 October. Available at: https://wwd.com/business-news/media/the-sound-of-music-7994307/ (Accessed: 3 October 2023).

Sotheby's (2020a) *Jeff Koons-Dom Pérignon Balloon Venus*. Available at: https://www.sothebys.com/en/buy/auction/2020/contemporary-art-day-an-online-auction/jeff-koons-dom-perignon-balloon-venus (Accessed: 6 March 2022).

Sotheby's (2020b) *Sotheby's to auction a singular, one-of-a-kind sneaker by adidas and Meissen: THE ZX8000 PORCELAIN*, 1 December. Available at: https://www.sothebys.com/en/press/sothebys-to-auction-a-singular-one-of-a-kind-sneaker-by-adidas-and-meissen-the-zx8000-porcelain (Accessed: 24 March 2022).

Spellings, S. (2021) "Beyoncé wears more than 200 carats of diamonds in a new Tiffany campaign", *Vogue*, 23 August. Available at: https://www.vogue.com/article/beyonce-jay-z-tiffany-campaign (Accessed: 5 March 2022).

Terrill, A. (2012) "David Lynch as Dom Pérignon's dark knight", *Elle*, 22 June. Available at: https://www.elle.com/culture/career-politics/news/a16700/david-lynch-as-dom-perignon-dark-knight/ (Accessed: 2 October 2023).

The Editors of Artnews (2021) "The Macallan's latest masterpiece: auction and collaboration of the ages", *ARTnews*, 22 March. Available at: https://www.artnews.com/art-news/sponsored-content/the-macallan-artist-collaborations-12345861 (Accessed: 27 February 2022).

Tiffany & Co. (2021) *About Love*. Available at: https://www.tiffany.com/stories/guide/beyonce-and-jay-z-about-love/ (Accessed: 5 March 2022).

Yotka, S. (2020a) "'A moment of sharing': Jonathan Anderson unpacks Loewe's show-in-a-box and 24-hour livestream", *Vogue*, 10 July. Available at: https://www.vogue.com/article/jonathan-anderson-unpacks-loewe-show-in-a-box-24-hour-livestream (Accessed: 6 March 2022).

Yotka, S. (2020b) "With a 'Show on the Wall,' Loewe delivers a jolt of fashion to your doorstep", *Vogue*, 1 October. Available at: https://www.vogue.com/article/loewe-spring-2021-show-on-the-wall (Accessed: 6 March 2022).

Zargani, L. (2020) "Miuccia Prada teams with five artists", *WWD*, 14 July. Available at: https://wwd.com/fashion-news/fashion-scoops/miuccia-prada-teams-with-five-artists-1203676741/ (Accessed: 6 March 2022).

2 Place

Places are more than predetermined and inert geographical entities: they are ongoing spatial creations emerging from the ways individuals, groups, institutions and businesses engage with their natural and socioeconomic environment (Escobar, 2001; Guthey, Whiteman and Elmes, 2014). Purposeful activities sustained in time – politics, education, religion, manufacturing, trade, leisure etc. – usually lead to the establishment of venues with a specific function and clearly defined boundaries, which spatially reflect the principles, the scopes and the acts shaping those activities. If stability consolidates places, human mobility and other social changes reconfigure their geography, obliterating redundant sites and generating new areas of aggregation and pursuit (Simmel, 1998).

As for luxury, in late medieval Europe its appreciation and consumption used to be secluded within the royal courts and the palaces of the aristocracy, as a prerogative of their exclusive lifestyle. With the development of overseas mercantile routes and the expansion of consumer cities, luxury started spreading across urban areas in the form of tradable commodities: from the 17th century, high-end goods found their place in boutiques and department stores, where they were put on display for the old and new wealth to purchase, and for the rest to gaze at (Miller, 1981; Benjamin, 1999; Dimant, 2009; Fujioka and Pitkänen, 2020).

Commercial venues notwithstanding, in the middle of 18th century luxury stores "began to assume a more decorative appearance" (Sombart, 1967, p. 110), and this would characterise the aesthetics of the luxury retail environment ever since. From architecture to fixtures, in a luxury boutique colours, shapes and materials are carefully arranged to echo and magnify the exquisite excellence of the goods on sale. This principle is also reflected in the products' merchandising, which tends to conform to the display codes of museums and art galleries (Petrov, 2019): a small selection of items is showcased on plinths or in glass cases, at a distance from each other and under "the soft light of an individual spotlamp" (Sudjic, 2009, p. 144). Besides signalling the square-foot opulence of the brand or retailer, the resulting "conspicuous emptiness" (Chayka, 2020, p. 111) draws an artistic aura around their goods.

DOI: 10.4324/9781003274094-3

Despite being presented as artworks in stores, luxury products have been for quite some time precluded access to cultural venues, especially in the case of fashion pieces by commercially active brands or designers. Contentious was the Yves Saint Laurent exhibition organised by Diana Vreeland in 1983 during her curatorial tenure at the Metropolitan Museum of Art (Vänskä and Clark, 2018; McCartney and Tynan, 2021): at the time, fashion curation itself was considered "a benign tumor" (Koda, in Tomkins, 2013) among the museum departments. Twenty years later, the Armani retrospective at the Guggenheim of New York stirred a heated debate about the "parasitic" (Sudjic, 2001) reliance of fashion on art, with fashion exhibitions being labelled as "assaults on the hallowed spaces of art" (Breward, 2003).

The terms "tumor", "parasitic" and "assault" well convey the rejective attitude of the museal establishment towards contemporary fashion pieces entering their space (Bauman, 2000). This, in turn, seemed to resonate with the emplacement culture of the medieval times, which was based on the hierarchical opposition – and the consequent spatial separation – among the different spheres of life (Foucault, 1986). Stemming from collectors' private cabinets, in Western societies museums represented the undisputed repositories of their intellectual and artistic patrimony as contrasted to the stores, mundane sites of business. As such, museums had retained throughout time an elitarian approach towards both the public they catered to and the objects or themes that, by admitting into their space, they would validate as culturally relevant (McLean, 1995; Codeluppi, 2003; Guilbaut, 2015). The Armani exhibition is a case in point that as late as the early 2000s the museal space had not been "desanctified" yet (Foucault, 1986, p. 23): fashion was still a foreign body in the field of haute-culture (Bourdieu, 1993a).

In just a few years, however, not only would the *museal ban* on luxury fashion be lifted, but the same concept of retail came to be featured in exhibitions (Petrov, 2019). In 2007, a fleeting store was arranged within the Takashi Murakami's retrospective at the Museum of Contemporary Art (MOCA) in Los Angeles, offering the fashion pieces he designed for the collaboration with Louis Vuitton and related monogrammed canvases (Fairs, 2007; Bengtsen, 2018). For the Japanese artist the pop-up store was meant to "incorporate the 'act of selling' into the exhibition as a performance" (Murakami, in Boehm, 2011); for Louis Vuitton, this and other similar initiatives placed the products outside the retail setting, generating an entirely "new atmosphere" (LV Internet Manager, in Riot, Chamaret and Rigaud, 2013, p. 931) around them. Similarly, in 2019 Virgil Abloh set up the Church & State room as part of his *Figures of Speech* exhibition at the Museum of Contemporary Art Chicago (MCA) (Sayej, 2019): located on the fourth floor, hence accessible only to ticket holders, the room hosted 20 re-edited fashion pieces available for purchase (Sayej, 2019; Brannigan, 2019). As its name suggests, Church & State playfully reflected the Foucauldian concept of emplacement, "draw[ing] attention to the false separation" (Brannigan, 2019) between the disinterested contemplation of objects in a museum – the "Church" – and the secular act of purchase in a shop – the "State".[1]

In the present days the debate about fashion acceptance in museums has become "irrelevant" (Strickland, 2014). With the neoliberal emphasis on the market and its accelerated circulation of objects, people and ideas, postmodernity has fuelled the proliferation of "places of transit and consumption" (Nodari, 2017, p. 37) such as the shopping centre, the hotel room, the supermarket and the airport.[2] This has deeply transformed how human beings inhabit places at large: while the spatial togetherness of individuals is much more determined by scope rather than by long-term relational intents, their engagement with a place is increasingly developing alongside the spectacular consumption of objects and contents (Debord, 1994; Featherstone, 2007; Baudrillard, 2017).

This postmodern commodification of space eventually steers towards the "functional de-differentiation" (Rectanus, in Ryan, 2007, p. 14) of places. As provocatively anticipated by Andy Warhol, whereas museums host exhibitions and related merchandise in collaboration with consumer brands (Codeluppi, 2003; Guilbaut, 2015; Sciolino, 2021) – morphing from gatekeepers of high culture into "hypermarket[s] of culture" (Baudrillard, 1982, p. 8) or "hypermuseums" (Guerisoli, 2018, p. 84), luxury boutiques are aptly evolving into spaces of hedonic elevation through the introduction of non-commercial features such as art installations and cultural programmes (Joy et al., 2014; Degen, 2023). A similar ratification process – here not explored further – interests also luxury places of transition like high-end hotels and executive airport lounges (Plaza Premium First, 2019; LaTour and Joy, 2022).

More widely, the synergies and cross-pollinations between luxury brand and art are articulating a novel spatial code, pinning the presence of luxury on the evolving conceptual and geographic map of today's consumers.

Designing luxury stores as heterotopias of wonder

Counterbalancing their market expansion and the growing volume of the merchandise released, since the 1990s luxury brands have intensified strategies to reenchant their retail space through the inclusion of art as a way to reinstate the exclusivity and uniqueness of luxury products on sale – albeit at a sensorial level (Vukadin, Lemoine and Badot, 2016; Crewe, 2018). The present-day luxury store thus appears a true heterotopia, "a floating piece of space" (Foucault, 1986, p. 27) with a traceable location and yet somehow unreal in its blending together the two opposing worlds of the commercial and the aesthetic.

The store's heterotopic presence is typically announced through a signature building, which dramatically interrupts the surrounding architectural landscape: the white minimalism of the New York Armani store designed by Peter Marino in 1996 contrasts with the characteristic brownstones of the

Upper East Side (Potvin, 2009); architecture firm Herzog & de Meuron included in their Tokyo Prada Epicenter a public plaza, a European feature quite distinctive from the plot-filling, space-efficient Japanese edifices (Mehta and MacDonald, 2011).

The architects and studios enlisted for luxury retail projects tend to be involved at various levels with cultural and artistic institutions: Peter Marino is the chairman of Venetian Heritage, a philanthropic organisation for the safeguard and promotion of Venice's artistic patrimony (Pelloux, 2019); Herzog & de Meuron designed the Switch House, the latticed brickwork extension of the Tate Modern in London (Stevens, 2016). The credentials of these starchitects thus percolate to their retail buildings elevating them to become "talismans of cultural capital" (Sharr, 2016, p. 167). Oftentimes it is their hallmark design style that draws a visible *fil rouge* between the luxury and the cultural projects in their portfolio: in 2019, firstly dubbed "starchitect" Frank Gehry roofed the Louis Vuitton Maison Seoul with sweeping glass sails, nodding to the weaving structure of his Fondation Louis Vuitton (Astbury, 2019); the deconstructed, angular dynamism of Las Vegas' Crystals at CityCenter luxury shopping mall by Studio Libeskind directly references their distinctive Jewish Museum in Berlin (Sharr, 2016).

Store windows cut through the building as a liminal space suspended "between the store's fantasy and street reality" (Cuito in Crewe, 2016, p. 521): behind the windows, products and decorative fixtures are creatively laid out to lure the passerby with an imaginative rendition of the offerings inside. At times creatives and artists harness the theatrical potential of the store window to generate self-standing, glass-enclosed utopias: to commemorate friend Alexander McQueen, in 2011 artist and celebrity Daphne Guinness turned the front window of Barneys New York into a stage for a one-off performance, where Guinness undressed behind a sheer screen to subsequently reappear in a stunning McQueen's gown (Richards, 2019); in occasion of her collaboration with Louis Vuitton one year later, Yayoi Kusama took over Selfridges' windows in London turning them into tridimensional canvas to reproduce *infinity mirror rooms* of primary colours and polka-dotted patterns (McCartney and Tynan, 2021).

While making a statement in the external environment, luxury retail buildings circumscribe an environment of their own (Sudjic, 2009). As mentioned above, the contemporary luxury retail space is being organised to favour artistic infusion by contiguity, whereby "luxury products bathe in an artistic ambiance so that artistic properties will infuse and contaminate them" (Dion and Arnould, 2011, p. 512). Besides the aforementioned museological merchandising of the items (Logkizidou et al., 2019), luxury brands have introduced in boutiques bona fide art pieces, firstly in areas aside from the selling floor, and subsequently populating the entire retail space (Manlow and Nobbs, 2013).

The incorporation of art, however, transcends matters of décor and serves now as a powerful statement of the cultural credibility luxury brands have accrued in the creative field (Bourdieu, 1993b). Former actresses and founders of fashion brand The Row, Ashley and Mary-Kate Olsen have established a solid relationship with Dakin Hart, senior curator of the Noguchi Museum, which has allowed them to borrow two Isamu Noguchi sculptures for their installation at Dover Street Market New York in 2018 (Garage Magazine, 2018) and three for their London boutique (Schneier, 2021). In 2018, Victoria Beckham hosted in her London flagship store a collection of Old Master artworks, lent by Sotheby's ahead of their Old Master Paintings sale (Finch, 2018).

Oftentimes, the art pieces displayed in store are ad hoc commissions. Such is the case of the collectibles designed in 2020 by Daniel Arsham for Dior, where the artist applied his *fictional archaeology* technique to corrode a selection of objects from Maison's archives and Christian Dior's personal possessions – a telephone, a clock, a basketball, a sculptural rendition of Dior's 1951 biography *Je suis couturier* etc. (Diderich, 2020). Inspired by the colourful vases of Yves Saint Laurent's Moroccan villa Jardin Majorelle, Saint Laurent's creative director Anthony Vaccarello commissioned specialist Mathilde Martin with a pottery edit for their Rive Droit boutique in Paris, the Los Angeles store and the online retail outlet (Socha, 2021). For the launch of the Alexander McQueen Pre-Fall 2022 collection, former creative director Sarah Burton displayed in store original artworks by 12 female artists, each one interpreting a look of the collection (Van Meter, 2022a). Celine has formalised its retail commissions under the initiative Celine Art Project, which now comprises site-specific works by over 40 emerging artists (Quick, 2021).

Whether borrowed or commissioned, the inclusion of in-store art has had a ripple effect, prompting luxury brands to rethink the nature and function of the retail space all together. Eponymous brand founder Victoria Beckham and Loewe's Jonathan Anderson, for instance, treat the boutique as a gallery space, adaptive to and constantly evolving along the art they host at a certain moment (Finch, 2018; Socha, 2020). This curatorial approach, in turn, reconfigures the dialogue between visitors and objects as it unfolds in store. For Anderson, in meandering through glass panels and glancing over fashion items and craftworks, visitors in Loewe boutiques undertake a journey of discovery: "it is almost as though you were turning the store into a TV set and stepping into a different world" (Anderson, in Socha, 2020).

This reflects more broadly the shift of postmodern consumption from the purchase of products to the enjoyment of experiences (Sepe, 2018): whilst material possessions are easily comparable, experiences retain a certain degree of perceived uniqueness, which stems from the personal – hence irreplicable – interaction of the individuals with their surrounding environment in the act of experiencing (Gilovich, Kumar and Jampol, 2015; Jing Daily, 2022). Even a store visit is now charged with an experiential cachet, as confirmed by recent reports of more than a half of global Gen Z shoppers heading to physical stores for a "fun experience" (Chitrakorn, 2022) rather than to satisfy a purchase need. In this context, luxury stores have evolved into heterotopian universes of aesthetic wonder, effacing the spatial and conceptual boundaries not only between artworks and luxury products but also between creation and consumption: the Ferragamo concept store in Soho New York functions as a "collaborative hub" (Van Meter, 2022b) for visitors to create their own digital artwork by customising NFTs by art producer Shxpir; Marni's store in Shanghai encloses a rock-like studio for in-residence artists, a "vessel for creativity" (Moss, 2022b) with windows and door opening directly into the store.

Together with reconfiguring their extant retail spaces luxury companies are creating novel typologies of experiential places: such is the case of AP Houses by Audemars Piguet, a network of secluded venues offering VIP clients a line-up of cultural events – from art exhibitions to musical performances (Highsnobiety, 2022) – and the Maisons Baccarat in Paris and Moscow, imagined by architect Philippe Starck as a cluster of other-worldly microcosms – the museum, the restaurant and the store – all gravitating around the theme of the alchemy behind glass-making (Starck, 2008).

Differently from the heterotopias of deviation and crisis of the past societies, i.e., places designed to isolate and contain conditions and behaviours deemed abnormal or noncompliant (Lévi-Strauss, 1974; Foucault, 1986), the contemporary boutiques emerge as heterotopias of wonder, emplacing in a spectacular fashion the "[un]limited permutations of retail, entertainment and service products" (Riewoldt and Hudson, 2000, p. 132) that characterise our experience of consumption.

Localism and nomadism of luxury spaces

In implementing their retail reenchantment strategy on a global scale, luxury brands seem to have gradually shifted from the uniformity principle of the early 2000s, by which they would recreate a consistent universe in all their stores, to "counter-standardisation" (Solca, in Sherman, 2022), whereby the stylistic references of each outlet are sourced in loco.

The Louis Vuitton Maison Osaka Midosuji pays tribute to Osaka's mercantile tradition: designed by architect Jun Aoki and decorated by Peter Marino, the metal fretwork motif at the ground level of the building and the white airy façade recreate a sailing *higaki-kaisen*, the regional characteristic cargo-vessel; the seafaring metaphor continues inside, with the wooden floors and metal ceilings sustained by wood-clad pillars evoking an on-board atmosphere (Mehta, 2020). For the Hermès boutique in Troy, Michigan, local multidisciplinary artist Ellen Rutt produced *Chain of Events*, a mural about the journey of human life that intertwines Hermès' iconography with the Great Lakes' natural landscape (Artnet News, 2021). In their work for Acne Studios' Parisian boutique, architectural firm Arquitectura-G relied on the locally sourced Saint Maximin creamy limestone as a trait d'union between the store and other Parisian landmarks like the Louvre and Place de la Concorde. This architectural dialogue with the urban surroundings is furthered by floor-to-ceiling windows: "[it] takes the soul of the city and brings it inside the store" (Arquitectura-G, in Moss, 2022a).

Luxury beauty brand Aesop has been at the forefront of the artistic localisation of their retail network, so much so that a section of their website, "Taxonomy of Design", details the provenance of the designers, fixtures and materials featured in each outlet (Aesop, 2022). It is, however, the geographic and socio-cultural milieu of the individual store that provides the springboard for the ambience design and the in-store initiatives. A relevant instance is the Aesop store in Georgetown, a neighbourhood in Washington, D.C., with a strong African-American heritage: the store has become the seat of the Aesop's Georgetown Spotlight, a programme for BIPOC creatives that has recently been unveiled with the work of local film photographer Donovan Gerald (Aesop, 2021; Aesopskincare, 2022). Whilst being its own world, the luxury boutique of today is hence a *porous heterotopy with deep local roots*.

Local artists have also been enlisted to personalise the iterations of luxury brands' mobile exhibitions. From 2015 through 2017 the *Wanderland* exhibition of Hermès travelled to London, Paris, Turin, Dubai, Seoul and Shanghai. Inspired by the concept of "*flânerie* (aimless city wandering)" (Benjamin, 1999), the 11 thematic rooms of the exhibition introduced the visitors to quintessential Parisian locations – a café, a metro station, the arcades, etc. – artistically reinterpreted through objects from the collection of Émile Hermès and the company's archives as well as through site-specific works of contemporary local creatives, such as those by Chinese mythology-inspired Wen Na and British graffiti artist CEPT, respectively featured in the Shanghai and London *Wanderland* iterations (Lyssens, 2015; Shanghai Daily, 2017).

With the aim to diversify their presence, in situ luxury brands are also experimenting with unconventional set-ups. Bottega Veneta has recently engaged with spatial hacking: in Seoul, the Italian brand staged a pop-up installation, *The Maze* – reference to the dystopian reality of the acclaimed South Korean Netflix drama *Squid Game* – with soft sculptures in its iconic parakeet green (Barandy, 2021); during the Chinese New Year of 2022, the Italian brand took over the Chinese Great Wall with another green installation, this time adding augural wishes in a tangerine hue (Pearl, 2022).

In occasion of the Saint Laurent's Spring/Summer 2022 fashion show on the Venetian island of Certosa artist Doug Atkin realised *Green Lens*, a plant-filled catwalk whose ten reflective prongs multiply the foliage generating a luxuriant forest. After the show *Green Lens* was left for a while as a temporary installation (Englefield, 2021). A similar concept lies behind Burberry's pop-up store on Jeju Island, South Korea. Part of the Imagined Landscapes, a world-wide retail project dedicated to the British house's outerwear, the Jeju Island store stands as a topographical shiny sculpture mirroring the surrounding mountainscape while hosting inside cinematic immersive art-works inspired by the great outdoors and the natural elements (WA Contents, 2021): through the imperfect reflections of its surface and the digital simula-tions hosted inside, the Burberry's pop-up store simultaneously dilates and transfigures the received sense of place of Jeju Island.

In all these projects the involvement of luxury brands rises above the mere exploitation of places as scenic backdrops, extending to the tutelage of each site's geo-historical heritage: Bottega Veneta and Saint Laurent have respec-tively pledged a donation for the maintenance of the Shanhai Pass on the Chinese Great Wall and for the restoration of the cloister ruins on Certosa. In Jeju Island Burberry established a five-year partnership with the Jeju Olle Foundation with the aim "to preserve the island's natural beauty and allow continued access for the public" (WA Contents, 2021).

The different spatial formats deployed by luxury brands point to their growing penchant for a more dynamic and creative geographical interaction with the audience. Quite similarly to the nomadic sovereigns constantly trav-elling across their loosely defined realms to tangibly manifest their power (Geertz, 2000), in order to maintain their appeal among an increasingly mo-bile and discerning customer base, luxury brands are now in constant need to travel around the world with exhibitions or to make themselves physically manifest in unusual places or through original venue arrangements. In this framework, the inclusion of local art and the reference to the surrounding natural and cultural landscape create a further layer of enrichment where the authenticity of the terroir and the unique spirit of the place are magnified into spectacularised localism.

The augmented geography of the art fair

As previously mentioned with museum exhibitions, the access of luxury brands to art and cultural venues as well as the ways they inhabit such un-related places is not always immediate nor linear, but it unfolds alongside the changing nature and scope of those venues. The evolution of the art fair as a spatial entity and its links with luxury brands is another relevant case in point.

Art fairs fully established themselves as trade platforms for art dealers and gallerists in the post-war period (Morgner, 2014). Still geographically restricted to specific European cities, in a few decades art fairs have grown exponentially in number and reach, passing from less than ten Western loca-tions in the 1980s to a staggering 200 and counting by 2012, spread across previously peripheral art market regions like Latin America, India and Asia (Schultheis et al., 2015). This geographic expansion also involved specific players, notably Frieze London and Art Basel: since the early 2000s, the two contemporary art fairs have created an international portfolio under their namesake brand, with Frieze franchising in New York, Los Angeles and recently Seoul, and Art Basel opening in Miami Beach, Hong Kong and Paris in 2022 – which de facto replaces FIAC, the International Contemporary Art Fair (Jhala, 2022a; Jhala, 2022b).

Most importantly, Frieze and Art Basel have paved the way towards the eventisation of art fairs by laying out a rich string of affiliated programmes and initiatives that cater to their heterogeneous audience – from private receptions for collectors to public talks; from VIP bespoke parties to educational guided tours. This added layer of "entertainment" (Gerlis, 2021, p. 14) has enlarged the scope of attendance to the fair beyond the mere appreciation and commerce of artworks with a new emphasis on networking (Morgner, 2014), as in the words of art dealer and curator Jeffrey Deitch: "in terms of Frieze, I'm more interested in the social connections. [...] The art fairs are informational, but it's a social platform" (Deitch, in Avins, 2022).

The morphed function of the art fair as a place-event attracting a wider footfall of art cognoscenti as well as affluent amateurs with a growing participation of millennials and Gen Zers has prompted luxury corporations to further explore collaborative opportunities beyond sponsorship (Langer, 2021).

In actual fact, the presence of luxury sponsors in the precincts of the art fairs has been conventionally limited to what Art Basel's former global director Marc Spiegler summarised as "a logo and a lounge" (Spiegler, in Rivetti and Gerlis, 2015), according to the principle that the floor "[is] for galleries who have earned it" (Spiegler, in Seligson, 2015). In the face of a circumscribed appearance on the floor, a few luxury companies have worked behind the scenes to synergise their art fairs' sponsorships with other patronage activities, in order to earn a bigger place in the art world as champions of the arts. Global associate partner of Art Basel since 2013, Audemars Piguet curated until 2019 their Collectors Lounges in Basel, Hong Kong and Miami Beach with commissioned art pieces commemorating its origins in the Jura Mountains (Audemars Piguet, 2023). The Swiss watchmaker also established Audemars Piguet Contemporary, an in-house curated art programme whose outputs are exhibited in major venues like the Venice Biennale and the West Bund Art & Design Fair in Shanghai (Brara, 2021).

Similarly, Ruinart leverages its rich champagne sponsorship portfolio of 35 among art fairs and events to showcase their Carte Blanche commission projects (Mun-Delsalle, 2020): like the camouflage pieces of Liu Bolin described in Chapter 1, the participatory installation by Jeppe Hein, Carte Blanche artists of 2022, has toured the Venice Biennale, Gallery Weekend Berlin, Art Brussels, Frieze London and New York, Art Basel Basel, Miami Beach, Paris+ par Art Basel and others (Ruinart, 2022).

Besides building their own artistic and cultural funding structure, in 2015 German marque BMW joined forces with Art Basel to establish the BMW Art Journey, a dedicated fund for the emerging artists of Basel Hong Kong to support their travels of research, network and inspiration (Banks, 2020; BMW Art Journey, 2023).

The cultural stimulation and the sense of "collective excitement" (Schultheis et al., 2015, p. 25) emanating from art fairs radiate to the hosting cities, "lend[ing] these locations the corresponding creative, fashionable and international flair" (Schultheis et al., 2015, p. 38). It is in this extended, carnivalesque environment that art fairs periodically create and recreate around them that most luxury brands settle in with their own satellite places and events.

For Art Basel Miami Beach and Miami Art Week 2021, lifestyle media brand Highsnobiety set up the HIGHArt Museum, a pop-up store featuring limited-edition artworks and apparel items curated by Highsnobiety founder David Fischer with Colette former owner Sarah Andelman and Art Basel's head of brand and creative Jeanne-Salomé Rochat (Barker, 2021). During Frieze Los Angeles 2022, Matches Fashion rented a mid-century house within the Trousdale Estate of Beverly Hills to serve as a private shopping venue and location for fashion parties (Avins, 2022). Organised as an itinerant "club that augments and extends significant global cultural gatherings at diverse locations worldwide" (Prada, 2022), Prada Mode landed to Art Basel Miami Beach 2018 offering cultural sideshows like DJ sets, art exhibits and an in-conversation panel about the role of the image in art and fashion.

Some brands establish their own place: such is the case of *Five Echoes*, a labyrinthic installation on show during the Miami Art Week 2021 that was commissioned by Chanel to British stage designer Es Devlin in occasion of the 100th anniversary of perfume Chanel N°5 (Parkes, 2021), or the ephemeral beachfront gallery erected by Saint Laurent for the same kermesse to display 55 sunrise paintings by Japanese artist Sho Shibuya, also celebrating the 55th anniversary of the first Rive Gauche boutique (Vogel, 2021).

In some other cases luxury brands creatively blend in the local landscape by reinterpreting landmarks or distinctive urban features. The 11th Street Diner is a renowned touristic attraction of Miami Beach as well as a meeting point for the locals. For the Miami Art Week 2019, Bottega Veneta took over the diner wrapping it in gold and personalising straws, napkins and salt-and-pepper shakers (Shim, 2019). With the nomadic project *Librairie Éphémère*, Louis Vuitton put a spotlight on newsagents as places of socialisation and intellectual exchange: in concomitance with relevant art events, local newsagent kiosks are restored and stocked with the Maison's region-specific publications (Bozino-Resmini, 2022). Iterations so far have involved the Parisian *bouquinistes* of the Rive Gauche during the Festival Photo, the Shanghai newsagents during the West Bund Art & Design Fair and the Venetian *edicole* during the Biennale (Bozino-Resmini, 2022).

The augmented geographies generated by art fairs and their syncretic prongs with luxury brands actualise curator Germano Celant's envision of culture as commodity: "in the end it all fits together: art, fashion, architecture, design – even shopping. It's all theatre, really. A modern spectacle for a modern world" (Celant, in Guilbaut, 2015, p. 7).

CASE

La Galerie Dior and the creation of a new consumption ecosystem

La Galerie is a place [...] blending tradition, adaption and modernity – so we know where we come from. Dior is now the only brand in our world which has this sort of space.

(Pietro Beccari [CPP-Luxury, 2022])

In 2018 Dior's newly appointed CEO Pietro Beccari undertook the renovation of the Maison's headquarters and historic flagship store in 30 Avenue Montaigne. Built in the 1860s as *hôtel particulier* for a son of Napoleon, 30 Montaigne became in 1946 Christian Dior's primary office and atelier for its proximity to the Hôtel Plaza Athénée and its eminent guests (Serafin, 2022).

As part of the ambitious refurbishment project, Beccari also factored in the creation of a permanent exhibition space to celebrate the life of Christian Dior, the artistic links and cultural influences informing his vision of couture, and the evolution of the Maison through the stylistic inputs of its seven creatives directors. Occupying the adjacent four-storey building in 11bis Rue Francois 1ᵉʳ, La Galerie Dior displays over 13 concept rooms, a rotating collection of documental materials, pictures, couture gowns, atelier toiles and accessories (CPP-Luxury, 2022).

The ambience design of La Galerie was commissioned to Nathalie Crinière, former interior architect at Centre Pompidou and scenographer for a previous project of the Maison (Allgeier, 2022). At the time of Beccari's request Crinière had just completed the installations for *Christian Dior: Designer of Dreams*, the exhibition launched in 2017 at the Musée des Arts Décoratifs (MAD) in Paris for the house 70th anniversary (LVMH, 2017), which would be followed by blockbuster iterations in London, Doha and New York (Harris and da Silva, 2019; Serafin, 2022).

A YouTube documentary about the Paris exhibition released by Dior during the pandemic (Christian Dior, 2020) describes Crinière's work to recreate at MAD the emblematic places of Dior's history – an art gallery, the atelier in 30 Montaigne, a boudoir, a garden etc. – dramatising them through artistic and artisanal atmospherics, from audio-visual effects to handmade paper-flower decorations. The creation of such an immersive and imaginative environment aimed to glorify Dior's creations stimulating the viewers' aesthetic appreciation of dresses and accessories beyond their commodity-function (Lezama, 2019): "couture isn't art; it's applied art. But when it's executed at the level, with the perfection, we see here, and displayed so gloriously, it has the effect of art: it can move you deeply" (Arthurboehm, 2020).

Whilst the magnificent chimeric language of the *Designer of Dreams* exhibition was replicated for the installations of La Galerie Dior, the space in Rue Francois 1ᵉʳ was reorganised to provide access to the historic rooms of the contiguous 30 Montaigne building – namely, Dior's office, the wood-panelled changing *cabine* of the models and the staircase taking them to the Grand Salon for the in-house fashion shows (Allgeier, 2022). When it came to the display of the dresses, Crinière also abandoned the museological conventions and showed most of the creations at the level of the viewer and without any glass panel, striking an intriguing balance between the aesthetic distance of the ambience and the experiential closeness to the objects on display: "it's an intimate way of visiting an exhibition [...]. You're really face to face with the clothing and the archival materials" (Crinière, in Allgeier, 2022).

Considerations

Together with 30 Montaigne, La Galerie Dior feeds into Dior's strategic reformulation of their landmark spaces to reflect the spectacular, multifaceted nature of postmodern consumption.

The same flagship store has been reconfigured beyond its primary retail function with areas allocated to service and hospitality – a suite, a spa, a restaurant and a pastry bar. Similar to the aforementioned Jonathan Anderson, flagship decorator Peter Marino has envisioned the customer's store visit not in transactional terms, but as an overarching experiential tour into the universe of Dior, "a walk through spaces that tells a story, that keeps the customer engaged and emotionally connected with Dior from start to finish" (Marino, in Serafin, 2022). In order to activate the customers' sensorial interaction with the brand, Marino commissioned site-specific artworks referencing Dior's history and themes, like the collage by Guy Limone integrating archival Dior photos, or the floral video installation by media artist Jennifer Steinkamp nodding to the well-known interest of Monsieur Dior for gardens (Serafin, 2022).

La Galerie Dior further enhances Dior's spatial storytelling by offering to a larger audience the opportunity to enter another Dior universe, just a corner away from 30 Montaigne. In granting its visitors a view of the original rooms or the architectonic features of 30 Montaigne, La Galerie is actually releasing the site's intrinsic heritage capital accrued through multiple temporal layers: the eminent pluri-centennial couture tradition of Paris, the legendary venture of Christian Dior in the post-war years and the evolution of the Maison ever since.

Despite the display of archival pieces and the original ambiences of 30 Montaigne, La Galerie Dior is not a museum or a commemorative mausoleum: Crinière's space design turns La Galerie into a temporal heterotopia, where the narration of the Dior's origins and legacy is artistically reinterpreted and aesthetically transfigured. The Diorama is the display in ascending colour spectrum of 1874, 3D-printed accessories and mini-robes replicas of the Maison's iconic creations from the inception years to today (CPP-Luxury, 2022): here, it is not the chronological unfolding of the styles but the colourful, scenographic ensemble that generates the spectacle, mesmerising the visitors' eyes and their mobile cameras.

With La Galerie Dior and 30 Montaigne, Dior is thus formalising a new consumption ecosystem, where art collaborations and artistic displays are masterfully put into dialogue with the surrounding space not merely to reenchant their products; rather, they turn these venues into the ultimate consumption experience. Whether browsing through the store in 30 Montaigne or visiting La Galerie Dior, customers and the public buy into the historical roots of the brand's artistry and creativity, amplified and packaged through the dramatic stylistic codes and the spectacular semantics of postmodernity.

Notes

1 During the 2022 iteration of the exhibition at the Brooklyn Museum of New York, visitors lined since early morning to access the Church & State room in the hope to get hold of the sought-after lime green Off-white X Nike Air Force 1 sneakers. Ironically, most would end up settling on Abloh's ordinary memorabilia – tote bags, mugs, posters, etc. (Lee, 2022).

2 These places were initially labelled "non-places" (Augé, 1995) to underline their weak connectivity (Aime, 2019a; Aime, 2019b) as opposed to the relational depth of "anthropological places" (Augé, 1995, p. 51), i.e., places endowed with character through the profound and direct bond individuals establish with each other and the place (Beidler and Morrison, 2016). With time the critique has acknowledged that postmodern individuals still retain a "need for places" (Augé, 2017, p. 10), i.e., the urge to make spatial sense of their lives. From this perspective, the contemporary globalised world is a far cry from being "placeless" (Massey, 2012, p. xiii): rather, the geography of postmodernity appears to be just more fragmented and heterogenous, including conventional anthropological places as well as digital spaces of connection and relation – e.g., social media – spaces with multilayered functionalities – e.g., cafés selling artworks and multi-faith prayer rooms in shopping centres – or new territories altogether – e.g., the metaverse and the web 3.

Bibliography

Aesop (2021) *Donovan Gerald*. Available at: https://www.aesop.com/uk/r/aesop-georgetown-donovan-gerald/ (Accessed: 18 August 2022).

Aesop (2022) *Taxonomy of Design*. Available at: http://taxonomyofdesign.com/#!/ (Accessed: 18 August 2022).

Aesopskincare (2022) *Making space for underrepresented art at Aesop Georgetown*, 9 February [Instagram]. Available at: https://www.instagram.com/p/CZw6Y7vMoQ2/?utm_source=ig_embed&ig_rid=f5082aab-2dc1-4900-acc2-979c49f32b3e (Accessed: 17 August 2022).

Aime, M. (2019a) *Comunità*. Bologna: il Mulino.

Aime, M. (2019b) "Prefazione: un ponte tra ieri e oggi", in M. Augé and J.P. Colleyn, *L'antropologia del mondo contemporaneo*. Translated by G. Lagomarsino. Milano: Elèuthera, pp. 7–16.

Allgeier, W. (2022) "Fashion and art: La Galerie Dior", *Gagosian Quarterly*, 22 March. Available at: https://gagosian.com/quarterly/2022/03/22/interview-fashion-art-la-galerie-dior/ (Accessed: 3 September 2022).

Arthurboehm (2020) *Couture isn't art; it's applied art* [YouTube]. Available at: https://www.youtube.com/watch?v=FLWDWzMrkBE&t=601s (Accessed: 24 October 2022).

Artnet News (2021) "Hermès lends a Detroit-based artist a platform at their new store in Troy, Michigan", *Artnet News*, 27 September. Available at: https://news.artnet.com/style/hermes-troy-store-2013077 (Accessed: 15 August 2022).

Astbury, J. (2019) "Frank Gehry crowns Louis Vuitton Maison Seoul with glass sails", *Dezeen*, 25 November. Available at: https://www.dezeen.com/2019/11/25/louis-vuitton-maison-seoul-frank-gehry-peter-marino/#:~:text=Frank%20Gehry%20has%20perched%20a,interiors%20by%20architect%20Peter%20Marino (Accessed: 3 July 2022).

Audemars Piguet (2023) *Our partnership with Art Basel*. Available at: https://www.audemarspiguet.com/com/en/about/audemars-piguet-contemporary/art-basel.html (Accessed: 7 October 2023).

Augé, M. (1995) *Non-places: Introduction to an Anthropology of Supermodernity*. Translated by J. Howe. London: Verso Books.

Augé, M. (2017) *Saper toccare*. Translated by F. Nodari. Milano: Mimesis edizioni.

Avins, J. (2022) "Fashion finds its place at Frieze Los Angeles", *Business of Fashion*, 21 February. Available at: https://www.businessoffashion.com/articles/luxury/fashion-finds-its-place-at-frieze-los-angeles/?utm_source=newsletter_dailydigest&utm_medium=email&utm_campaign=Daily_Digest_210222&utm_content=intro (Accessed: 30 May 2022).

Banks, N. (2020) "How brands can benefit from arts patronage, BMW Culture Lead Thomas Girst explains", *Forbes*, 25 June. Available at: https://www.forbes.com/sites/nargessbanks/2020/06/25/bmw-art-basel-ninth-art-journey/?sh=2d5fe5413a2e (Accessed: 15 October 2022).

Barandy, K. (2021) "Explore Bottega Veneta's immersive, green MAZE installation in Seoul", *Designboom*, 20 October. Available at: https://www.designboom.com/architecture/bottega-veneta-immersive-parakeet-green-maze-installation-seoul-korea-10-20-2021/ (Accessed: 17 May 2022).

Barker, T. (2021) "Our HIGHArt Museum store without the museum is officially open in Miami", *Highsnobiety*, 1 December. Available at: https://www.highsnobiety.com/p/highart-miami-pop-up/ (Accessed: 30 May 2022).

Baudrillard, J. (1982) "The Beaubourg-effect: implosion and deterrence", translated by R. Krauss and A. Michelson, *October*, 20, pp. 3–13.

Baudrillard, J. (2017) *The Consumer Society: Myths and Structures*. London: Sage Publications.

Bauman, Z. (2000) *Liquid Modernity*. Cambridge: Polity Press.

Beidler, K.J. and Morrison, J.M. (2016) "Sense of place: inquiry and application", *Journal of Urbanism: International Research on Placemaking and Urban Sustainability*, 9/3, pp. 205–215. Available at: https://doi.org/10.1080/17549175.2015.1056210.

Bengtsen, P. (2018) "Fashion curates art: Takashi Murakami for Louis Vuitton", in A. Vänskä and H. Clark (eds.) *Fashion Curating: Critical Practice in the Museum and Beyond*. London: Bloomsbury Academic, pp. 199–212.

Benjamin, W. (1999) *The Arcades Project*. Translated by H. Eiland and K. McLaughlin. Cambridge: The Belknap Press of Harvard University Press.

BMW Art Journey (2023) *BMW Art Journey*. Available at: https://bmwartjourney.com/ (Accessed: 7 October 2023).

Boehm, M. (2011) "MOCA customer settles suit against Vuitton over Murakami canvases", *Los Angeles Times*, 5 March. Available at: https://www.latimes.com/ entertainment/la-xpm-2011-mar-05-la-et-murakami-suit-20110305-story.html (Accessed: 19 June 2022).

Bourdieu, P. (1993a) *Sociology in Question*. Translated by R. Nice. London: Sage Publications.

Bourdieu, P. (1993b) *The Field of Cultural Production: Essays on Art and Literature*. Translated by various hands. Cambridge: Polity Press.

Bozino-Resmini, M. (2022) "Le edicole storiche di Venezia si trasformano in librairie éphémère con Louis Vuitton", *Architectural Digest Italia*, 26 April. Available at: https://www.ad-italia.it/article/le-edicole-storiche-di-venezia-si-trasformano-in-librairie-ephemere-con-louis-vuitton/ (Accessed: 15 August 2022).

Brannigan, M. (2019) "The luxury evolution of the museum gift shop", *Fashionista*, 17 October. Available at: https://fashionista.com/2019/09/museum-gift-shops-luxury-retail (Accessed: 6 June 2022).

Brara, N. (2021) "'We're always looking for different perspectives': Audemars Piguet's in-house curators on the watchmaker's art commissions", *Artnet News*, 12 February. Available at: https://news.artnet.com/art-world/audemars-piguet-curators-interview-1942708 (Accessed: 15 October 2022).

Breward, C. (2003) "Shock of the frock", *The Guardian*, 18 October. Available at: https://www.theguardian.com/artanddesign/2003/oct/18/art.museums (Accessed: 19 June 2022).

Chayka, K. (2020) *The Longing for Less: Living with Minimalism*. New York: Bloomsbury Publishing.

Chitrakorn, K. (2022) "From Jacquemus to Balenciaga: luxury fashion brands go hyperphysical", *Vogue Business*, 4 May. Available at: https://www.voguebusiness.com/ consumers/from-jacquemus-to-balenciaga-luxury-fashion-brands-go-hyperphysical-retail (Accessed: 7 July 2022).

Christian Dior (2020) *"Christian Dior, Designer of Dreams" at the Musée des Arts Décoratifs*, 14 April [YouTube]. Available at: https://www.youtube.com/ watch?v=FLWDWzMrkBE&t=601s (Accessed: 15 September 2022).

Codeluppi, V. (2003) *Il Potere del Consumo*. Torino: Bollati Boringhieri.

CPP-Luxury (2022) "Dior is opening in Paris 'La Galerie Dior', a living museum of the brand", *CPPLuxury*, 9 March. Available at: https://cpp-luxury.com/dior-is-opening-in-paris-la-galerie-dior-a-living-museum-of-the-brand/ (Accessed: 19 September 2022).

Crewe, L. (2016) "Placing fashion: art, space, display and the building of luxury fashion markets through retail design", *Progress in Human Geography*, 40/4, pp. 511–529. Available at: https://doi.org/10.1177/0309132515580815.

Crewe, L. (2018) *The Geographies of Fashion: Consumption, Space and Value*. London: Bloomsbury Academic.

Debord, G. (1994) *Society of the Spectacle*. Translated by K. Knabb. London: Rebel Press.

Degen, N. (2023) *Merchants of Style: Art and Fashion After Warhol*. London: Reaktion Books.

Diderich, J. (2020) "Dior taps Daniel Arsham for limited-edition art objects", *WWD*, 5 March. Available at: https://wwd.com/fashion-news/fashion-scoops/dior-taps-daniel-arsham-limited-edition-art-objects-1203531800/ (Accessed: 3 July 2022).

Dimant, E. (2009) "From 'paradise' to cyberspace: the revival of the bourgeois marketplace", in J. Potvin (ed.) *The Places and Spaces of Fashion, 1800-2007*. New York: Routledge, pp. 232–246.

Dion, D. and Arnould, E. (2011) "Retail luxury strategy: assembling charisma through art and magic", *Journal of Retailing*, 87/4, pp. 502–520. Available at: https://doi.org/10.1016/j.jretai.2011.09.001.

Englefield, J. (2021) "Doug Aitken creates kaleidoscopic catwalk for Saint Laurent show in Venice", *Dezeen*, 15 July. Available at: https://www.dezeen.com/2021/07/15/doug-aitken-green-lens-saint-laurent/ (Accessed: 18 August 2022).

Escobar, A. (2001) "Culture sits in places: reflections on globalism and subaltern strategies of localization", *Political Geography*, 20, pp. 139–174. Available at: https://doi.org/10.1016/S0962-6298(00)00064-0.

Fairs, M. (2007) "Louis Vuitton 'fleeting store' at MOCA by Jean Marc Gady", *Dezeen*, 11 October. Available at: https://www.dezeen.com/2007/10/11/louis-vuitton-fleeting-store-at-moca-by-jean-marc-gady/ (Accessed: 17 May 2022).

Featherstone, M. (2007) *Consumer Culture and Postmodernism*. London: Sage Publications.

Finch, M. (2018) "Victoria Beckham: modern muse among the masters", *Sotheby's*, 22 June. Available at: https://www.sothebys.com/en/articles/victoria-beckham-modern-muse-among-the-masters?locale=en (Accessed: 19 June 2022).

Foucault, M. (1986) "Of other spaces", translated by J. Miskowiec, *Diacritics*, 16/1, pp. 22–27.

Fujioka, R. and Pitkänen, J. (2020) "Department stores and luxury business", in P.Y. Donzé, V. Pouillard and J. Roberts (eds.) *The Oxford Handbook of Luxury Business*. Oxford: Oxford University Press, pp. 333–351.

Garage Magazine (2018) "The Row is bringing a Noguchi show to Dover Street Market", *Garage*, 6 September. Available at: https://garage.vice.com/en_us/article/ev7gge/the-row-noguchi-dover-street (Accessed: 3 July 2022).

Geertz, C. (2000) *Local Knowledge: Further Essays in Interpretive Anthropology*. New York: Basic Books.

Gerlis, M. (2021) *The Art Fair Story: A Rollercoaster Ride*. London: Lund Humphries.

Gilovich, T., Kumar, A. and Jampol, L. (2015) "A wonderful life: experiential consumption and the pursuit of happiness", *Journal of Consumer Psychology*, 25/1, pp. 152–165. Available at: http://dx.doi.org/10.1016/j.jcps.2014.08.004.

Guerisoli, F. (2018) "Contemporary art and urban attractiveness: the role of hypermuseums and art foundations", in M. Paris (ed.) *Making Prestigious Places: How Luxury Influences the Transformation of Cities*. London: Routledge, pp. 81–91.

Guilbaut, S. (2015) "Museum ad nauseam? Museums in the post-modern labyrinth", *Perspective: Actualité en histoire de l'art*, 2, pp. 1–13. https://doi.org/10.4000/perspective.6078.

Guthey, G.T., Whiteman, G. and Elmes, M. (2014) "Place and sense of place: implications for organizational studies of sustainability", *Journal of Management Inquiry*, 23/3, pp. 254–265. Available at: https://doi.org/10.1177/1056492613517511.

Harris, G. and da Silva, J. (2019) "Dior show smashes total attendance record at the V&A – but Alexander McQueen exhibition had more daily visitors", *The Art Newspaper*, 3 September. Available at: https://www.theartnewspaper.com/2019/09/03/dior-show-smashes-total-attendance-record-at-the-vandabut-alexander-mcqueen-exhibition-had-more-daily-visitors (Accessed: 4 September 2022).

Highsnobiety (2022) "Inside AP House, Audemars Piguet's exclusive new lounge", *Highsnobiety*, 13 May. Available at: https://www.highsnobiety.com/p/audemars-piguet-mark-ronson-song-ap-house/ (Accessed: 27 July 2022).

Jhala, K. (2022a) "Frieze reveals the 118 galleries taking part in its inaugural Seoul fair", *The Art Newspaper*, 29 June. Available at: https://www.theartnewspaper.com/2022/06/29/frieze-announces-the-118-galleries-taking-part-in-its-inaugural-seoul-fair-this-september (Accessed: 15 October 2022).

Jhala, K. (2022b) "Art Basel announces galleries for its inaugural Paris fair – we look at how it compares with last year's FIAC list", *The Art Newspaper*, 12 July. Available at: https://www.theartnewspaper.com/2022/07/12/art-basel-announces-galleries-for-its-inaugural-paris-fair-compares-with-fiac (Accessed: 15 October 2022).

Jing Daily (2022) "Why real-life experiences help sell hard luxury to China's Gen Z", *Jing Daily*, 13 January. Available at: https://jingdaily.com/why-real-life-experiences-help-sell-hard-luxury-to-chinas-gen-z/ (Accessed: 15 August 2022).

Joy, A., Wang, J.J., Chan, T.S., Sherry, J.F. Jr. and Cui, G. (2014) "M(Art) worlds: consumer perceptions of how luxury brand stores become art institutions", *Journal of Retailing*, 90/3, pp. 347–364. Available at: http://dx.doi.org/10.1016/j.jretai.2014.01.002.

Langer, D. (2021) "Art Basel Hong Kong: how artists are being energised by luxury brands looking to captivate social-savvy Gen Z", *Style*, 20 May. Available at: https://www.scmp.com/magazines/style/news-trends/article/3134196/art-basel-hong-kong-how-artists-are-being-energised (Accessed 30 May 2022).

LaTour, K.A. and Joy, A. (2022) "The artification of hospitality: elevating service to luxury status", in A. Joy (ed.) *The Future of Luxury Brands: Artification and Sustainability*. Berlin: De Gruyter, pp. 265–286.

Lee, A.G. (2022) "The thirst of merch", *The New York Times*, 6 July. Available at: https://www.nytimes.com/2022/07/06/style/virgil-abloh-museum-merchandise.html (Accessed: 30 July 2022).

Lévi-Strauss, C. (1974) *Tristes Tropiques*. Translated by J. Weightman and D. Weightman. New York: Atheneum Books.

Lezama, N. (2019) "Re-thinking luxury in the museum fashion exhibition", *Luxury: History, Culture, Consumption*, 6/1, pp. 83–104. Available at: https://doi.org/10.1080/20511817.2020.1738708.

Logkizidou, M., Bottomley, P., Angell, R. and Evanschitzky, H. (2019) "Why museological merchandise displays enhance luxury product evaluations: an extended art infusion effect", *Journal of Retailing*, 95/1, pp. 67–82. Available at: https://doi.org/10.1016/j.jretai.2018.11.001.

LVMH (2017) *"Christian Dior, Designer of Dreams"*: Maison Dior showcased at Musée des Arts Décoratifs to celebrate 70ᵗʰ anniversary, 5 July. Available at: https://www.lvmh.com/news-documents/news/christian-dior-designer-of-dreams-maison-dior-showcased-at-musee-des-arts-decoratifs-to-celebrate-70th-anniversary/ (Accessed: 9 September 2022).

Lyssens, S. (2015) "Strolling in an Hermès Wanderland", *Wallpaper*, 9 April. Available at: https://www.wallpaper.com/fashion/strolling-in-an-hermes-wanderland (Accessed: 18 August 2022).

Manlow, V. and Nobbs, K. (2013) "Forms and function of luxury flagships: an international exploratory study of the meaning of the flagship store for managers and customers", *Journal of Fashion Marketing and Management*, 17/1, pp. 49–64. Available at: https://doi.org/10.1108/13612021311305137.

Massey, D. (2012) "Preface", in I. Convery, G. Corsane and P. Davis (eds.) *Making Sense of Place: Multidisciplinary Perspectives*. Woodbridge: The Boydell Press, pp. xiii–xiv.

McCartney, N. and Tynan, J. (2021) "Fashioning contemporary art: a new interdisciplinary aesthetics in art-design collaborations", *Journal of Visual Art Practice*, 20/1–2, pp. 143–162. Available at: https://doi.org/10.1080/14702029.2021.1940454.

McLean, F. (1995) "A marketing revolution in museums?", *Journal of Marketing Management*, 11/6, pp. 601–616. Available at: https://doi.org/10.1080/02672 57X.1995.9964370.

Mehta, M. (2020) "Louis Vuitton opens new flagship store in Osaka, inspired by sailing vessels", *Stirworld*, 7 February. Available at: https://www.stirworld.com/see-news-louis-vuitton-opens-new-flagship-store-in-osaka-inspired-by-sailing-vessels (Accessed: 7 June 2022).

Mehta, G. and MacDonald, D. (2011) *New Japan Architecture: Recent Works by the World's Leading Architects*. North Clarendon: Tuttle Publishing.

Miller, M.B. (1981) *The Bon Marché: Bourgeois Culture and the Department Store, 1869-1920*. London: George Allen & Unwin.

Morgner, C. (2014) "The evolution of the art fair", *Historical Social Research*, 39/3, pp. 318–336. Available at: https://doi.org/10.12759/hsr.39.2014.3.318-336.

Moss, J. (2022a) "Acne Studios' new Paris store combines classicism and counter-culture", *Wallpaper*, 22 June. Available at: https://www.wallpaper.com/fashion/acne-studios-new-paris-store-rue-st-honore-opens?utm_source=Selligent&utm_medium=email&utm_campaign=20220623_XWP-X_NWL_EO_Daily-Digest&utm_content=20220623_XWP-X_NWL_EO_Daily-Digest&utm_term=8793155&m_i=RD%2B_mmE1bWEHLX4YsNPlkikNe6ta1b2B84Ag4xu07PnRwEcVwHiJDg_9 9fN70kJLp2Og25UhmGalSve5bPefwmQnZ8RiFPRRRR&lrh=3d8c79b3364f9758 b36d74eaccf9b416214d8f3fb4e6a092d9684146bfdeb5c3&M_BT=38661145981656 (Accessed: 15 August 2022).

Moss, J. (2022b) 'Step into the greatest fashion boutiques in the world', *Wallpaper*, 22 July. Available at: https://www.wallpaper.com/fashion/virtual-tour-of-the-worlds-best-designed-boutiques?utm_source=Selligent&utm_medium=email&utm_campaign=20220722_XWP-X_NWL_EO_Daily-Digest&utm_content=20220722_XWP-X_NWL_EO_Daily-Digest&utm_term=8793155&m_i= %2B9RbHGSRQQHzkw%2BFgq4YX1OgxeX5abRsnVZ_hQtmOTe0ZTXaJbr5 MK35ZsmUAAszdNaWmSDoe2YIIVoK4aO5zhJ9xk87WzP%2B%2Ba&lrh=3 d8c79b3364f9758b36d74eaccf9b416214d8f3fb4e6a092d9684146bfdeb5c3&M_ BT=38661145981656 (Accessed: 8 August 2022).

Mun-Delsalle, Y.J. (2020) "Q&A with Frederic Dufour, President and CEO of Ruinart", *Forbes*, 4 June. Available at: https://www.forbes.com/sites/yjeanmundelsalle/2020/06/04/qa-with-frederic-dufour-president-and-ceo-of-ruinart/?sh=1830bcea56e9 (Accessed: 16 October 2022).

Nodari, F. (2017) "L'autore", in M. Augé, *Saper toccare*. Translated by F. Nodari. Milano: Mimesis edizioni, pp. 37–43.

Parkes, J. (2021) "Es Devlin creates labyrinth in Miami to celebrate 100 years of Chanel no 5", *Dezeen*, 16 December. Available at: https://www.dezeen.com/2021/12/16/es-devlin-five-echoes-labyrinth-chanel-miami/ (Accessed: 30 May 2022).

Pearl, D. (2022) "Bottega Veneta hosts a brand takeover on the Great Wall of China", *Business of Fashion*, 11 January. Available at: https://www.businessoffashion.com/news/luxury/bottega-veneta-hosts-a-brand-takeover-on-the-great-wall-of-china/ (Accessed: 18 August 2022).

Pelloux, C. (2019) "An inspiring conversation with art and architecture Maestro Peter Marino", *Forbes*, 2 December. Available at: https://www.forbes.com/sites/ceciliapelloux/2019/12/02/an-inspiring-conversation-with-art-and-architecture-maestro-peter-marino/?sh=577105f11da0 (Accessed: 20 September 2022).

Petrov, J. (2019) *Fashion, History, Museums: Inventing the Display of Dress*. London: Bloomsbury Visual Arts.

Plaza Premium First (2019) *Immersive Art Experience at Gallery In-Lounge by Plaza Premium First*. Available at: https://www.plazapremiumfirst.com/news/poly-art (Accessed: 7 August 2022).

Potvin, J. (2009) "Armani/architecture: the timelessness and textures of space", in J. Potvin (ed.) *The Places and Spaces of Fashion, 1800-2007*. New York: Routledge, pp. 247–263.

Prada (2022) *Prada Mode Miami*. Available at: https://www.prada.com/us/en/pradasphere/events/2018/prada-mode-miami.html (Accessed 24 October 2022).

Quick, H. (2021) "The Celine Art Project: how art and ideas shape the world of Celine stores", *Sotheby's*, 8 October. Available at: https://www.sothebys.com/en/articles/a-meeting-of-minds-hedi-slimane-explores-the-fine-art-of-style (Accessed: 24 July 2022).

Richards, J. (2019) "Transcending the traditional: fashion as performance", in F. Carlotto and N.C. McCreesh (eds.) *Engaging with Fashion: Perspectives on Communication, Education and Business*. Leiden: Brill, pp. 249–257.

Riewoldt, O. and Hudson, J. (2000) *Retail Design*. London: Laurence King Publishing.

Riot, E., Chamaret, C. and Rigaud, E. (2013) "Murakami on the bag: Louis Vuitton's decommoditization strategy", *International Journal of Retail & Distribution Management*, 41/11–12, pp. 919–939. Available at: https://doi.org/10.1108/IJRDM-01-2013-0010.

Rivetti, E. and Gerlis, M. (2015) "Beyond the VIP lounge: art fair sponsorship steps up a gear", *The Art Newspaper*, 18 December. Available at: https://www.theartnewspaper.com/2015/12/18/beyond-the-vip-lounge-art-fair-sponsorship-steps-up-a-gear (Accessed: 6 October 2023).

Ruinart (2022) *Jeppe Hein*. Available at: https://www.ruinart.com/en-gb/jeppehein.html (Accessed: 15 October 2022).

Ryan, N. (2007) "Prada and the art of patronage", *Fashion Theory*, 11/1, pp. 7–24. https://doi.org/10.2752/136270407779934588

Sayej, N. (2019) "Virgil Abloh's latest drops can only be copped via museum", *Garage*, 6 June. Available at: https://garage.vice.com/en_us/article/evym37/virgil-abloh-museum (Accessed: 6 June 2022).

Schneier, M. (2021) "Beige Ambition", *The Cut*, 2 March. Available at: https://www.thecut.com/2021/03/mary-kate-ashley-olsen-the-row.html (Accessed: 3 July 2022).

Schultheis, F., Single, E., Egger, S. and Mazzurana, T. (2015) *When Art Meets Money: Encounters at the Art Basel*. Translated by J. Fearns. Köln: Verlag der Buchhandlung Walther König.

Sciolino, E. (2021) "The Louvre turns to merch", *The New York Times*, 3 March. Available at: https://www.nytimes.com/2021/03/03/style/louvre-uniqlo-merch.html (Accessed: 24 June 2022).

Seligson, H. (2015) "The brands in Art Basel's orbit", *The New York Times*, 7 March. Available at: https://www.nytimes.com/2015/03/08/business/the-brands-in-art-basels-orbit.html (Accessed: 9 October 2022).

Place 45

Sepe, M. (2018) "Experiencing prestigious places: contemporary forms and modalities", in M. Paris (ed.) *Making Prestigious Places: How Luxury Influences the Transformation of Cities*. London: Routledge, pp. 59–71.

Serafin, A. (2022) "Past meets present: inside 30 Avenue Montaigne, Dior's new look Parisian flagship", *Wallpaper*, 19 August. Available at: https://www.wallpaper.com/fashion/dior-30-avenue-montaigne-paris-store-museum?utm_source=Selligent&utm_medium=email&utm_campaign=20220407_XWP-X_NWL_EO_Daily-Digest&utm_content=20220407_XWP-X_NWL_EO_Daily-Digest&utm_term=8793155&m_i=FCwv6UGZZcoKIL7ruSixKRMRGL51518dYlE%2BiFGPNfQyDpt0c1mfkOEbt5gzlwFkSBAtWonbE7VQEBZ9BEHVRNhsGrZvNSaFFE&lrh=3d8c79b3364f9758b36d74eaccf9b416214d8f3fb4e6a092d9684146bfdeb5c3&M_BT=38661145981656 (Accessed: 23 August 2022).

Shanghai Daily (2017) "Wander through the wonders of Hermès", *Shanghai Daily.com*, 23 April. Available at: https://archive.shine.cn/feature/events-and-tv/Wander-through-the-wonders-of-Herms/shdaily.shtml (Accessed: 18 August 2022).

Sharr, A. (2016) "Libeskind in Las Vegas: reflections on architecture as a luxury commodity", in J. Armitage and J. Roberts (eds.) *Critical Luxury Studies: Art, Design, Media*. Edinburgh: Edinburgh University Press, pp. 151–176.

Sherman, L. (2022) "What makes a luxury store successful", *Business of Fashion*, 4 July. Available at: https://www.businessoffashion.com/articles/retail/what-makes-a-luxury-store-successful/ (Accessed: 30 July 2022).

Shim, B. (2019) "Golden Bottega Veneta diner opens its doors during Art Basel Miami Beach", *Designboom*, 8 December. Available at: https://www.designboom.com/design/golden-bottega-veneta-diner-art-basel-miami-beach-12-07-2019/ (Accessed: 7 October 2023).

Simmel, G. (1998) *Sociologia*. Translated by G. Giordano. Torino: Edizioni di Comunità.

Socha, M. (2020) "Jonathan Anderson says stores must offer 'unique discoveries'", *WWD*, 4 December. Available at: https://wwd.com/business-news/retail/jonathan-anderson-loewe-paris-store-1234668128/ (Accessed: 3 July 2022).

Socha, M. (2021) "Saint Laurent dabbles in ceramics", *WWD*, 16 August. Available at: https://wwd.com/fashion-news/fashion-scoops/saint-laurent-ceramics-vaccarello-1234899249/ (Accessed: 3 July 2022).

Sombart, W. (1967) *Luxury and Capitalism*. Translated by W.R. Dittmar. Ann Arbor: The University of Michigan Press.

Starck (2008) *Maison Baccarat, Moscow*, 1 January. Available at: https://www.starck.com/maison-baccarat-moscow-p1989 (Accessed: 8 October 2022).

Stevens, P. (2016) "Tate Modern's Switch House expansion by Herzog & de Meuron set to open in London", *Designboom*, 24 May. Available at: https://www.designboom.com/architecture/herzog-de-meuron-tate-modern-switch-house-london-05-24-2016/ (Accessed: 6 October 2023).

Strickland, K. (2014) "Fashion as art? Galleries think so", *The Australian Financial Review*, 25 October. Available at: https://www.proquest.com/newspapers/fashion-as-art-galleries-thinkso/docview/1748838751/se-2?accountid=13958 (Accessed: 12 May 2022).

Sudjic, D. (2001) "Is the future of art in their hands?", *The Guardian*, 14 October. Available at: https://www.theguardian.com/theobserver/2001/oct/14/2 (Accessed: 19 June 2022).

46 *Place*

Sudjic, D. (2009) *The Language of Things*. London: Penguin Books.

Tomkins, C. (2013) "Anarchy unleashed", *The New Yorker*, 18 March. Available at: https://www.newyorker.com/magazine/2013/03/25/anarchy-unleashed (Accessed: 19 June 2022).

Van Meter, W. (2022a) "Alexander McQueen creative director Sarah Burton asked 12 female artists to interpret her Pre-Fall collection, with intriguing results", *Artnet News*, 17 June. Available at: https://news.artnet.com/style/alexander-mcqueen-process-show-2132143 (Accessed: 3 July 2022).

Van Meter, W. (2022b) "Ferragamo launches a new Soho concept store featuring an interactive NFT collaboration with digital creator Shxpir", *Artnet News*, 28 June. Available at: https://news.artnet.com/style/ferragamo-2137422 (Accessed: 7 July 2022).

Vänskä, A. and Clark, H. (2018) "Introduction: fashion curating in the museum and beyond", in A. Vänskä and H. Clark (eds.) *Fashion Curating: Critical Practice in the Museum and Beyond*. London: Bloomsbury Academic, pp. 1–15.

Vogel, M. (2021) "With a beachfront gallery for artist Sho Shibuya's sunrise paintings, Saint Laurent Rive Droit makes a splash in Miami", *Artnet News*, 2 December. Available at: https://news.artnet.com/style/saint-laurent-sho-shibuya-art-basel-miami-beach-2042689 (Accessed: 17 October 2022).

Vukadin, A., Lemoine, J.F. and Badot, O. (2016) "Opportunities and risks of combining shopping experience and artistic elements in the same store: a contribution to the magical functions of the point of sale", *Journal of Marketing Management*, 32/9–10, pp. 944–964. Available at: https://doi.org/10.1080/0267 257X.2016.1186106.

WA Contents (2021) "Burberry creates topographic mirrored pop-up store on Jeju Island", *World Architecture*, 26 November. Available at: https://worldarchitecture.org/architecture-news/empmf/burberry-creates-topographic-mirrored-pop-up-store-on-jeju-island.html (Accessed: 18 August 2022).

3   Time

Together with space, time is the dimension defining human consciousness and its experience of the world. Just as places are socially constructed, time is also a "social artefact" (Martineau, 2016, p. 1) emerging from – and specific to – the way a certain civilisation formalises the patterns of occurrence, duration and pace of their events and practices, and its memory (Elias, 1992; Hassan, 2009; Aime, 2019).

In medieval societies, life related to the infinite time of God: human existence was considered a mere temporal parenthesis in the individuals' spiritual journey towards the ultimate redemption (Martineau, 2016); agrarian work and community rituals synchronised with the cyclical rhythm of the seasons, and were thus believed to manifest the eternal dimension of the Divine through "the return of the same here on earth" (Debord, 1994, p. 74). From the late Middle Ages (14th–16th centuries), the growth of urban centres as places of trade and consumption encouraged a worldlier approach to life focussed on the enjoyment of pleasures *hic et nunc* (here and now) rather than on the spiritual preparation for the afterlife (Sombart, 1967). In addition, studies in linguistics, archaeology and astronomy throughout the Renaissance and the Enlightenment period (15th–18th centuries) substantiated the gradual accumulation of knowledge and capabilities of humankind across time, opening the future to potential progress instead of surrendering it to the repetition of the same (Quinones, 1972; Whitrow, 1988; Van de Peer, 2014). In this way not only was the perpetual circularity of the time of God deconstructed into a linear sequence of dimensions – past, present, future – but these dimensions were also qualitatively incremental, with present and future transcending the past (Osborne, 1995). It is this secularised and possibilistic temporal horizon that accompanied the industrialisation and the technological development of the Western world.

Industrial capitalism validated time as a metric of economic performance, whereby productivity was assessed on the output produced within a specific interval of time. This approach historically built up on the clock-time of the late medieval merchants (Thompson, 1967; Quinones, 1972) made of homogenous, standardised and comparable units – days, hours, minutes – with the

DOI: 10.4324/9781003274094-4

addition of the speed factor: the quicker the goods are produced, the cheaper their cost; the faster they reach the marketplace, the larger the competitive advantage of the producer over their rivals (Adam, 2004; Hassan, 2009). Opposite to the immutable, otherworldly nature of the medieval time, capitalistic time is thus a "quantitative resource" (Adam, 1995, p. 100) that can be bought and exploited, needs to be efficiently optimised, and in no way must it be wasted (Weber, 2005).

From plants and factories, the tempo of industrial production gradually permeated all the other spheres of human life to become the overarching temporal principle governing our times: on this account, contemporary societies not only endow speed with a positive connotation – quick is good – but seem to have developed a real "'fetish' for speed" (Hassan, 2009, p. 19), unconditionally vouching for the quicker the better (Adam, 1995).

This is particularly evident in the realm of consumption, which is set on an acute "nexting" (Aime, 2019, p. 84), i.e., the relentless quest for new objects, contents and images. From a temporal perspective, novel goods subsume in themselves newness and nowness: by introducing a variation in the current offering, new products mark the existing ones as obsolete, hence drawing a temporal boundary between past and present that is redrawn at every novelty release (Buck-Morss, 1989). Apparel companies have been at the forefront of feeding the market's demand for the next new thing through the periodic output of fashionable clothes, i.e., items stylistically imbued with the allure of the now and whose "rapid lifecycle [is] dictated by the exhaustion of their fashionability quotient rather than of their material conditions" (Carlotto, 2023, p. 123).

Beyond the apparel industry, the generation of products grounded in trends has become one of the dominating commodity structures of the post-Fordist economy: in a context where the generation of value has shifted from scale to scope-variety (Salais and Storper, 1992), more companies in different sectors are looking to capitalise on the temporal cachet of the trend realising their profits through the constant supply of the *cool* item, the updated version, the latest novelty.

The adoption of a trend commodity structure, or "fashioni[s]ation" (Parguel, Delécolle and Mimouni Chaabane, 2020), has also involved luxury and art, which conventionally deal with rare, one-of-a-kind pieces.

Luxury products are perceived and presented as the output of time-intensive activities, from creative design to artisanal production (Carlotto, 2023). Pressured by a neophilic market and the quarterly timetable of the financial performance reporting, since the 1990s fashion brands under the big luxury conglomerates have accelerated their productive cycle: Louis Vuitton has mechanised the artisanal assembling of their handbags reducing the lead time from eight days to one day (Passariello, 2006); fashion brands have moved the calendar of their shows from a bi-seasonal to a monthly frequency, with an increased emphasis on industrial ready-to-wear lines over laborious, hand-made couture, and to the detriment of designers' creativity (Thomas, 2015; WWD Staff, 2015); in the last decade a few companies even shortened the customers' waiting time by adopting the "see-now-buy-now" format, where the items on the catwalk are immediately available to purchase (Carlotto, 2018).

Art business is also setting on the present as its main temporal coordinate. In the last 30 years, the focus of the art trade has been shifting from the Old Master paintings to contemporary art: contrary to the limited availability of Old Masters, *wet paint* ensures a continuous supply to titillate collectors' appetite, which leads to a growing volume of the transactions and a more dynamic market overall (Currid-Halkett, 2007; Adam, 2014). Artist and critic Grayson Perry thus captures the art world's enthusiasm for the new: "the world of art seems to be strongly associated with novelty. [...] Work is always 'cutting edge', artists are 'radical', shows are 'mould-breaking', ideas are 'ground-breaking', 'game-changing', 'revolutionary', a 'new paradigm' is forever being set" (Perry, 2016, p. 76). Art institutions are following suit: to attract a wider audience and secure their financial viability, museums have been turning to topics and aspects that reflect our current interests instead of just preserving and documenting the past.

It is within the framework of the new and the now that luxury brand and art collaborations sit: delving deeper into their temporal features, in any case, unveils a much more complex and dynamic network of temporalities, which ultimately echoes and feeds into the "timescape"[1] of postmodern consumption.

The digital now and its quantic moments

If postmodern societies live in a perpetual present (Firat and Venkatesh, 1995), advances in the Internet Communication Technologies (ICTs) have further accelerated our perception of it.

Almost fulfilling the famed motto of Facebook founder Mark Zuckerberg, "move fast and break things" (Zuckerberg, in Taplin, 2017, p. vii), by moving at the speed of light the Internet compresses time to the extent of fragmenting it into instants. In the resulting "flashing pointillism" (Simpson, 1995, p. 144) of moments that characterises the online environment, it is the intensity of each moment that assumes value over its actual duration: "instantaneity [...] makes every moment infinitely capacious; and infinite capacity means that there are no limits to what could be squeezed out of the moment – however brief and 'fleeting'" (Bauman, 2000, p. 182). From this perspective, the digital moment very much resembles a physical quantum, "a unit of action which contains energy and time" (Adam, 2004, p. 63).

The present on the Internet is thus a hyper-now constantly emerging from the real-time sequence of instants charged with content, like the feeds of Instagram or TikTok's video posts. In seamlessly integrating with our physical life, the digital hyper-now and its quantic moments have come to define the tempo of consumption as well: the more ephemeral the consumption environment becomes, the more every single instant defining consumers' encounter and engagement with the products will need to be dazzling and attention-grabbing (Bardhi and Eckhardt, 2017; Pine and Gilmore, 2019; Eckhardt and Bardhi, 2020).

The timeframe in which luxury brand and art collaborations are envisioned reflects the postmodern focus on novelty and present-ness, inclusive of its most recent quantic evolutions.

As considered in Chapter 1, many product-based collaborations consist in the artistic tweak of the known appearance of luxury items in terms of shape, colour, packaging etc. While some brands produce one standout version at a time – see the Macallan Anecdotes of Ages Collection and Dom Pérignon's limited editions – collaborative edits like the Dior Lady Art series and the Artycapucines Collection by Louis Vuitton multiply the newness quotient of the products by proposing each year simultaneous revisitations by different artists. Wrapped in a layer of newness yet still recognisable, these items capture and retain the attention of the consumers by playing with the perceptual overlap between the usual and the novel. It has to be noted, in addition, that each artistic tweak draws around the product the aura of uniqueness typical of the artwork, meant as the one-time output of a creative act taking place in specific circumstances (Sennett, 2009). Whilst being new, the artified luxury product is also timeless, abstracted from the short time span of the trend commodity and elevated to a collectible.

The timing in which new collaborations are unveiled can also leverage the spectacular capacity of the present moment. In 2021 Alexandre Benjamin Navet drew the second-skin case for each of Ruinart's four cuvées, in 100 pieces per cuvée. Ruinart released the editions at the frequency of one cuvée per week, from 7 June to 7 July (Ruinart, 2023): similar to the "drop model" adopted by many fashion companies, these weekly launches generated a series of micro-rituals around the launch, reactivating customers' excitement at each individual release (Baron, 2018).

In other cases the debut of a collaboration is enriched through simultaneous side initiatives. Undercover Spring/Summer 2020 collection co-designed by Jun Takahashi with photographer Cindy Sherman was launched just before the artist's solo show at the National Portrait Gallery (Allwood, 2019). Bottega Veneta's takeover of the 11th Street Diner during Art Basel Miami Beach 2019 (Chapter 2) coincided with the opening of their boutique in the Design District (Phelan, 2019). In May 2021 La Prairie presented at Frieze New York the video installation of their resident artist Carla Chan while sponsoring across town the *MoMA PS1* exhibition on multimedia artist Niki de Saint Phalle (Artnet News, 2021). Previous collaborative projects can also be given a brand-new life, such as the case of *My Heart that Blooms in the Darkness of the Night*, the floral sculpture designed in 2020 by Yayoi Kusama for Veuve Clicquot's vintage La Grande Dame 2012. In 2022, the work was repurposed at The Park at CityCenter in Washington, DC as part of a series of Veuve Clicquot-sponsored events paying homage to the Japanese artist, all coinciding with the renowned local cherry blossoming season (Elliott, 2022).

In addition to the continuous creation of artistically enhanced products and augmented launches, luxury brands rely on art to magnify the quantic energy of their ephemeral initiatives (Bardhi and Eckhardt, 2017). Besides its forays into spatial hacking with innovative artistic formats (Chapter 2), Bottega Veneta opened in 2021 a pop-up store in London's Shoreditch to showcase the newest Salon 02 collection together with art pieces by Greem Jeong, Daniel Gordon and Kwangho Lee, contributors to the brand's digital magazine *Issue 02* (Theodosi, 2021). Jimmy Choo adopted a similar approach for the Chinese debut of its Chasing Stars capsule collection, designed by the House creative director Sandra Choi with graffiti and graphic designer Eric Haze, and curated by Japanese fashion maestro Poggy. The power of the hyper-now in retail is confirmed by the fact that BE@RBRICK, the Chasing Stars collectible toy exclusively launched at The Hall pop-up store in Shanghai, was sold out just a few hours after the opening (Law, 2021). In 2019 Ruinart launched in London their second Ruinart 1729, a two-week, one-suite hotel whose ambience was decorated by Loewe's Jonathan Anderson with objects from his home and private collection (Parsons, 2019). As suggested by its name, the 24h Museum set up by Prada with media artist Francesco Vezzoli and Rem Koolhaas' practice AMO occupied the Parisian Palais d'Iéna on 24 February 2012, for merely one day. The 24h Museum was meant to explore the concept of femininity through visual and performative arts initiating "a collective rite that mixes visitors, red-carpet, Oedipus' complex and night visions" (Prada, 2012). In this ultra-transitory context even a *"rite"* does not hold any customary recurrence nor long-term social standing anymore, but its significance is both reduced to and intensified as a one-night spectacular gathering (Aime, 2019).

Unpacking and repackaging the past

With its emphasis on the intrinsic value of the instant, our era of the hyper-now tends to overlook the sequence of events and the link between cause and effect, which conceptually mark the passage of time (Elias, 1992). This ends up having far-reaching implications: first, it interrupts the succession of past, present and future, hence questioning the modern Western construct of the linearity of time (Fabris, 2003). In addition, it colonises the past dimension by subjecting it to an ancillary role towards the present (Hassan, 2009; Aime, 2019).

Whilst creatives and artists have often found inspiration in prior artworks, aesthetics and genres, a few recent collaborative projects shed light on the approach currently taken when drawing from the past.

Artistic director of Louis Vuitton's womenswear since 2013, Nicolas Ghesquière concocted for the Fall/Winter 2021 season a capsule edition with Italian atelier Fornasetti, reinterpreting and reproducing their distinctive heritage designs – architectural features, cameo portraits, antique coins etc. – onto clothing and accessories. The presentation of the collection was live streamed at the Louvre: the models walked amongst the ancient sculptures, sarcophaguses and bas-reliefs of the Michelangelo and Daru Galleries on the notes of a medley of hits by Daft Punk (Louis Vuitton, 2021).

If sourcing from Fornasetti's 13,000-piece archive (Socha, 2021a) had for Ghesquière "the excitement of an archaeological dig" (Ghesquière, in Madden, 2021), the collaboration as presented on the runway turned out to be an exercise in "aesthetic archaeolog[y]" (Hawkins, 2022b): the heritage designs of Fornasetti – artistic sublimations of ancient iconographies themselves – were blended with the bright colours and futuristic volumes of the garments, the electronic music of the 1990s and 2000s and the Roman, Greek and Etruscan antiquities, resulting in a cross-temporal tessellation of styles and suggestions.

Art-historical references in luxury design have been the subject of two collaborative exhibitions. In 2019, auction house Christie's launched *Art Adorned*, a private selling exhibition with paintings and decorative art from the Renaissance to the Rococo period displayed in thematic rooms alongside matching Dolce & Gabbana's couture and haute-jewellery items (Christie's, 2023). Earlier that year, Spanish shoe designer Manolo Blahník partnered with the Wallace Collection on the exhibition *An Enquiring Mind: Manolo Blahník at the Wallace Collection* and personally curated a selection of archival models to be featured with the museum's masterpieces according to the movement, theme or motif that inspired him (Wallace Collection, 2019).

In his review of *An Enquiring Mind*, art commentator Adrian Clark labels "painstaking" (Clark, 2019, p. 87) any attempt to establish a chronology of Blahník creations: instead, one needs to appreciate their aesthetic – albeit temporary – transfiguration within the splendid setting of the museum, as precious rarities enclosed in antique-esque glass bell jars or in cabinets among snuff boxes and other fine art objects. In the same way, the online video preview of *Art Adorned* centres on the *fil rouges* connecting the masterpieces on sale and the Dolce & Gabbana's creations, irrespective of any temporal order (Christie's, 2019). Here, it is the striking syncretism of the pairings that matters, as in the case of the lavish couture gown matched with a sacred painting by Bicci di Lorenzo not only for the bodice of the gown reproducing a Madonna by Domenico Ghirlandaio but also for the bright yellow ostrich feathers applied on the sleeves and the skirt, a daring rendition of the gold ground of the late Middle Ages paintings.

The archaeological imagery of Ghesquière as well as the temporal bricolage of the two collaborative exhibitions above profiled dramatise the fragmented nature of time past: in a postmodern context the past ceases to be a dimension to be explored or "a land to return to" (Appadurai, 2005, p. 30) and becomes a repository of images, suggestions and symbols that can be creatively appropriated and rearranged (Delanty, 2000).

As a matter of fact, past is very much made and remade in the present. This is particularly evident in the heritage storytelling of luxury brands, where brands do not go back to the past to merely reconstruct their history but they "go back while looking ahead" (Carlotto and Tanner, 2021, p. 174), retrieving and elaborating past-related cues to lure the current audience and ensure the brand's longevity in the future. As observed by La Galerie Dior's master-mind Pietro Beccari (Chapter 2): "tradition is there to be stretched, pulled and teased – to become, again and again, contemporary, fresh, stimulating and desirable" (Beccari, in Serafin, 2022).

A case in point is *Re-Signify Part One* by Valentino, a brand exhibition launched in 2020 at Shanghai's Power Station of Art that was followed one year later by a second chapter, *Re-Signify Part Two*, held at the SKP-S' T-10 space in Beijing. The *Re-Signify* series presented the Chinese audience with an immersive overview of the Maison's codes – the stud, the rose, haute cou-ture, the "V" logo etc. – explored through Valentino's archival creations in combination with contemporary artworks by Cao Fei, Xu Zhen, Jonas Mekas, Jacopo Benassi and others (Cleary, 2021).

Like Beccari, Valentino's creative director Pierpaolo Piccioli has a very contemporary approach to tradition: Piccioli defines his creative work as a re-signification process of the history of the Maison to imbue the brand with new meanings and currency (Valentino, 2023b). From this perspective, archives serve him not much "as historical pieces" but mostly as sources of "memory and inspiration" (Piccioli, in Zargani, 2020). With *Re-Signify* Valentino thus creates a "spectacular archive" for the audience "to walk through different moments of the Maison's history, not just in a chronological display but with an emotional involvement" (Valentino, 2023b). The dramatic display setting of Valentino's creations and the presence of artworks thus become the conduit for the audi-ence's sensorial engagement, which ultimately enables the Chinese public – most likely to feel spatially and temporally far from Valentino – "to project new possible realities" (Valentino, 2023a) around the brand.

Past-inspired collaborations are commonly defined as a "dialogue" (Koons, 2017; Wallace Collection, 2019; Louis Vuitton, 2021) between the contemporary creator and history. The closing moment of Ghesquière's Fall/Winter 2021 fashion show, with the last model standing still in front of the *Winged Victory of Samothrace* (Louis Vuitton, 2021), is a powerful reminder that in the postmodern era this dialogue, far from being relational, is purely spectacular. In the above collaborations as well as in the previously outlined Masters by Jeff Koons for Louis Vuitton and the historical mashup videos of Chanel and Tiffany (Chapter 1), the past is unpacked and repackaged into a sensorial and playful kaleidoscope of references. Resonating through reality and simulation, memories and reveries, nostalgia and escapism, the past thus becomes a commodity for aesthetic consumption in its own right.

The circular timing of traditions and anniversaries

Time comes, time passes and sometimes time returns. Besides collaborations embracing the capacity of the passing moment or the suggestive depth of the past, a number of projects and initiatives build up on the consistency of the circular time, developing around periodic occurrences and commemorations.

After a first isolated attempt in the 1920s, since 1945 winemaker Baron Philippe de Rothschild and his family successors at Château Mouton Rothschild have been commissioning artist-designed labels for their vintages on a yearly basis (Palumbo, 2019). Over the decades, the initiative has involved high-calibre contributors like Pablo Picasso, Salvador Dalí, Dorothea Tanning, George Braque, Wassily Kandinsky, Andy Warhol. In 1981 the collection of the Mouton Rothschild's art labels became the subject of a dedicated travelling exhibition, *Mouton Rothschild – Paintings for the Labels* (Château Mouton Rothschild, no date a), which eventually lead to the creation of a permanent Paintings for the Labels Room in 2013 (Château Mouton Rothschild, no date b).

It has been pointed out earlier that in product-based collaborations the artistic input provides luxury products with a fresh edge that speaks to the penchant of the postmodern market for novelty and surprise, while somehow positioning the products above it as unique items. The periodic iteration and the continuity in time, in addition, earn these collaborative initiatives further reputational credit, eventually consolidating them as time-honoured traditions. Building the perceptual association of Muton Rothschild with art year after year was for Baron de Rothschild a soft-power move to underline the unparalleled prestige of his wine, which his lobby campaign with the French government succeeded in formalising only in 1973 with the Premier cru reclassification (Joy et al., 2021). In addition, an impressive pedigree of illustrious predecessors can appeal to prospective collaborators: Olafur Eliasson, Muton Rothschild artist of 2019, accepted the commission because he wanted to be "part of a river. The many artists here are inspiring, as together they have shaped the river that I am now part of" (Eliasson, in Makris, 2022). One of the artists participating to the sixth edition of the Dior Lady Art project, British-Liberian Lina Iris Viktor similarly commented that besides the opportunity to widen her artistic domain, "it is equally gratifying to become part of a legacy of invited artists" (Portee, 2021).

Whilst the concept of tradition refers to continuity cemented in time, the anniversary is the point in time where that continuity is acknowledged and celebrated. The launch of an art collaboration can be an impactful format to mark a luxury brand's historical milestones.

In commemoration of the tenth year since Alexander McQueen's skull print scarf was first released, in 2013 Damien Hirst created with the British brand 30 limited-edition designs adapted from his Entomology series, which were featured in a short film by photographer Sølve Sundsbø (Braun, 2013; Vogue, 2013). The Fondation Pierre Bergé – Yves Saint Laurent celebrated the 60th anniversary of Saint Laurent through a multilocation show held in six Parisian museums. Similar to the *Art Adorned* and *An Enquiring Mind* exhibitions described above, the Maison's fashion creations and accessories were selected and displayed in each venue according to their specific atmosphere and character: abstract silhouettes and optical patterns matched with the artworks of the Centre Pompidou, while ornate, gilded items found their place in the sumptuous interiors of the Galerie d'Apollon at the Louvre (Hawkins, 2022a). *Louis Vuitton X* is a Los Angeles show organised in 2019 by the French Maison as a tribute to its 160 years of artistic collaborations: almost 200 archive collaborative pieces ranging from scarves to perfume bottles were displayed in ten thematic rooms, together with ad hoc commissions to Cindy Sherman, Frank Gehry and others (Cogley, 2019). The exhibition also served as a launch platform for the Artycapucines Collection, whose first six-piece edition was presented in a rainbow-hued display (Petras, 2019). As demonstrated by the layout and the ambience design, the focal point of *Louis Vuitton X* was not the historical succession of Louis Vuitton art projects, but the longue durée, i.e., the Maison's long-standing commitment to the arts, which in turn validated the debuting Artycapucines project as the latest instance in a centennial – hence respectable – string of partnerships.

Another relevant date in the anniversary calendar of Louis Vuitton was 4 August 2022, which marked the 200th year from the birth of eponymous founder Louis Vuitton. From that day throughout the rest of the year a series of initiatives were released under the collective banner "Louis 200": from the fictional novel *Louis Vuitton, L'Audacieux* published by leading French printing house Gallimard, to the Apple TV documentary *Looking for Louis*; from the trunk-themed store windows to the videogame app *Louis: The Game*, retracing young Louis' entrepreneurial journey (Socha, 2021b). Artists and creatives were called to work for "Louis 200" across a variety of formats: American painter Alex Katz realised a large-scale triptych portrait of Louis Vuitton; 200 contributors – including illustrator Jean-Philippe Delhomme, interior designer Pierre Yovanovitch, art director Willo Perron and architect Peter Marino – were called to reimagine the Maison's iconic trunk; digital artist Beeple designed ten out of 30 non-fungible tokens (NFTs) for *Louis: The Game* (Socha, 2021b; Block, 2021).

"Louis 200" is another instance of a collaborative project articulated as an ensemble programme of objects, contents and events (Chapter 1): in this case, more than a temporal theme, the birth anniversary of Louis Vuitton offered the French powerhouse the unique opportunity to enrich the origins of their corporate history by telling the story of the man behind the brand and bring it alive as a spectacular legend through a diverse mix of artistic activations.

CASE

Rooted in the time of the planet: *Retour Aux Sources* and Ruinart

When experiencing Retour aux Sources, the viewer is encouraged to question the role of mankind within nature and how interdependent our ecosystems must be.

(Ruinart, 2022b)

In 2029 Ruinart will celebrate their 300-year foundation anniversary. Since September 2019 the French champagne house has been carrying on the Countdown project, whereby each year an artist or a collective is entrusted with an artwork themed on sustainability (Mun-Delsalle, 2020a). The initiative has been defined by CEO Frédéric Dufour as an act of impatience: after commemorating its 290th year of activity in 2019 and unwilling to wait another decade until the tricentenary, Ruinart decided to mark the ten-year lead up time through artistic commissions that can "bring meaningful and fresh discoveries every year" (Dufour, in Mun-Delsalle, 2020b).

The kick-off work of the countdown series is *Retour Aux Sources*, an AI-driven visual and sound installation by digital creator Maya Mouawad and Cyril Laurier, musician and researcher in machine learning (Ruinart, 2019). *Retour Aux Sources* consists in a root structure with Murano glass bubbles hanging from its rhizomes. Positioned into one of Ruinart's crayères chalk cellars 30 metres underground, the root is connected to the vineyards above through a set of sensors. The sensors record and compare data about the geo-climatic surroundings – from the soil composition to the levels of the precipitation – as well as any variation involving the vineyards' environment throughout the stages of winemaking (Ruinart, 2022b).

Perpetually exposed to new data and feeding back to the records already stored, the root comes alive generating a unique series of light reflections and sound effects. The result is an immersive experience where the masterful blend of technological applications and human creativity captures the interaction between the flow of time and the spirit of the place, manifesting it to the senses as art.

Considerations

Ruinart's portfolio of artistic collaborations is fairly extensive. Originated in 1896 with an advertising poster commissioned to Czech illustrator Alphonse Mucha, in time the connections between the champagne house and the art world have increased and diversified with the establishment of yearly art programmes and prizes like Carte Blanche, Prix Maison Ruinart and Ruinart Studio, as well as with the patronage of art fairs and dedicated events around the world (Ruinart, 2022a). This requires Ruinart to synchronise with a variety of temporalities, from the hyper-now of retail with the product drops like the aforementioned Ruinart × Navet 2021 cuvées to the seasonal calendar of the sponsored art fairs, where also the final outputs of its art programmes are usually presented (Chapter 2).

Additionally, it must be noted that most of Ruinart's programmes have a clear focus on sustainability: Ruinart Studio is dedicated to the artistic upcycle of waste from the Maison's winemaking activities; the choice of the Carte Blanche artist is mainly based on their commitment on sustainability; the Countdown is meant to foster "the dialogue between art, nature and technology" (Ruinart, 2022a). By framing their artistic commissions through the lens of sustainability, Ruinart is actually setting its clock on an additional temporal framework: the time of the planet.

The time of the planet flows as an interdependent network of cycles of varying extent, duration and speed, linking together all the organisms in a certain ecosystem, and characterised by the entropic transfer, release or transformation of energy from one organism to another, from one cycle to another (Adam, 1994; Carlotto, 2023).

Appreciating the interconnected circularity of nature is of particular relevance to Ruinart, for winemaking is highly dependent on the distinctive correlation between the topography of the vineyards, their geo-climatic properties, the vintners' vision and the technological inputs that go into the process: in the words of artists Mouawad and Laurier, "it depends a lot on the weather and what nature can offer" (Mouawad and Laurier, in Mun-Delsalle, 2020a). Whilst it is this unique set of factors determining the primary characteristics of their champagnes, the actual colour, bouquet and taste of each vintage will depend on the unpredictable circumstances – an excessive heat or a drought season – impacting on the condition of the terroir that year (Joy et al., 2021).

Retour aux Sources presents an artistic rendition of the temporal ecology of Ruinart's winery in Reims. The crayères chalk cellars where the root is installed sit on one-million-year-old ocean floor sediments and were excavated thousands of years ago. Classified as a UNESCO World Heritage Site for their unique conformation, the cellars seem to be a "place where time stands still" (Ruinart, 2022b). This perceived immobilism, however, is just apparent: the cellars are in fact undergoing constant morphogenetic movements indiscernible to human eye, while calibrating the specific interaction among minerals, organic matter, microorganisms, air and water that characterises the soil of the vineyards. The AI-sensors allow the sentient root to make sense of these slow-paced changes in connection with faster, detectable cyclical processes like the seasonal changes and the annual lifecycle of the vines, as well as irregular and episodic events such as rain or cold waves.

By translating this complex symphony of rhythms into an artistic performance, *Retour aux Sources* leads the audience to the heart of the earth pulsing
through the sequence, order and pauses of the root's lights and sounds. Differently from the escapist time-travelling experiences explored above, the return
to the origins of *Retour aux Sources* is about connecting with the "multiple
rhythms of nature" (Adam, 1994, p. 76) – whether it is the geological era or
the daily weather change – and their holistic interplay, eventually inscribing
the finite human existence within it. Here, Mouawad and Laurier make purposeful use of technology as an enabling tool to reconnect human beings to
nature, thus taking distance from that modern Western narrative that would instead frame technology in antagonistic terms to nature (Mun-Delsalle, 2020a).

On a corporate scale, fine-tuning on the circular time of the planet offers
Ruinart an alternative framework to the unidimensional capitalistic time and
a blueprint for sustainable business. Instead of applying "a point-in-time
perspective" (Adam, 1995, p. 139) that looks at production as a linear process in which resources are sourced, managed and disposed solely in function of the final output, a circular approach adopts a "long-term thinking"
(Schumacher, 2011, p. 198) and considers each resource and stage of production bound to multiple, interconnected loops of different magnitude and
temporal breadth. This extends the corporate accountability beyond the final
output, urging the Maison to ensure the product's durability in time – "no
human product really lasts unless it is created with respect for its environment" (Ruinart, 2022b) – and to implement nature-like circular operations
like the Ruinart Studio upcycling programme, where waste is regenerated
and integrated back into other cycles of production and consumption.

Note

1 "Timescape" is a term coined by sociologist Barbara Adam to indicate "a cluster
of temporal features" (Adam, 2004, p. 143) defining the temporal relations in a
specific field. These temporal features include, among others, extension (duration),
sequence (cause and effect), patterns (periodicity and cyclicality), point (moment),
tempo (pace), frames (epochs, ages, days, seconds).

Bibliography

Adam, B. (1994) *Time and Social Theory*. Cambridge: Polity Press.
Adam, B. (1995) *Timewatch: The Social Analysis of Time*. Cambridge: Polity Press.
Adam, B. (2004) *Time*. Cambridge: Polity Press.
Adam, G. (2014) *Big Bucks: The Explosion of the Art Market in the 21st Century*. Lon-
don: Lund Humphries.
Aime, M. (2019) *Comunità*. Bologna: il Mulino.
Allwood, E.H. (2019) "Cindy Sherman appears on the runway at Undercover's
SS20 show", *Dazed*, 20 June. Available at: https://www.dazeddigital.com/fashion/
article/44940/1/artist-cindy-sherman-jun-takahashi-undercover-ss20-paris-fashion-
week (Accessed: 20 November 2022).

Appadurai, A. (2005) *Modernity at Large: Cultural Dimensions of Globalization*. Minneapolis: University of Minnesota Press.

Artnet News (2021) "For La Prairie, 2021 was defined by the beauty of art collaborations and a sense of blue", *Artnet News*, 13 December. Available at: https://news.artnet.com/art-world/la-prairie-2021-art-projects-2045881 (Accessed: 20 November 2022).

Bardhi, F. and Eckhardt, G.M. (2017) "Liquid consumption", *Journal of Consumer Research*, 44/3, pp. 582–597. Available at: https://doi.org/10.1093/jcr/ucx050.

Baron, K. (2018) "Digging into drop culture: evolving a roaring retail ritual", *Forbes*, 29 October. Available at: https://www.forbes.com/sites/katiebaron/2018/10/29/digging-into-drop-culture-evolving-a-booming-retail-ritual/?sh=77e529b577d8 (Accessed: 24 November 2022).

Bauman, Z. (2000) "Time and space reunited", *Time & Society*, 9/2–3, pp. 171–185. Available at: https://doi.org/10.1177/0961463X00009002002.

Block, F. (2021) "Louis Vuitton launches a video game to target young consumers", *Penta*, 4 August. Available at: https://www.barrons.com/articles/louis-vuitton-launches-a-video-game-to-target-young-consumers-01628109921 (Accessed: 22 December 2022).

Braun, M. (2013) "Daniel Hirst and Alexander McQueen collaboration", *Widewalls*, 15 November. Available at: https://www.widewalls.ch/magazine/damien-hirst-x-alexander-mcqueen (Accessed: 23 December 2022).

Buck-Morss, S. (1989) *The Dialectics of Seeing: Walter Benjamin and the Arcades Project*. Cambridge: The MIT Press.

Carlotto, F. (2018) "The fashion 'timescape': historical evolution and contemporary features", in F. Carlotto and N.C. McCreesh (eds.) *Engaging with Fashion: Perspectives on Communication, Education and Business*. Leiden: Brill, pp. 41–59.

Carlotto, F. (2023) "'In Search of Lost Time': luxury fashion's emerging circular initiatives and the shifting temporal features of fashion consumption", in A. Joy (ed.) *New Directions in Art, Fashion, and Wine: Sustainability, Digitalization, and Artification*. Lanham: Lexington Books, pp. 119–137.

Carlotto, F. and Tanner, A. (2021) "New old stories: the temporal landscape in Fortnum & Mason's digital heritage storytelling", in A. Sikarskie (ed.) *Storytelling in Luxury Fashion: Brands, Visual Cultures, and Technologies*. New York: Routledge, pp.174–189.

Château Mouton Rothschild (no date a) *Key Dates: 1981*. Available at: https://www.chateau-mouton-rothschild.com/the-history/key-dates/key-date-1981 (Accessed: 20 December 2022).

Château Mouton Rothschild (no date b) *The Paintings for the Labels Room*. Available at: https://www.chateau-mouton-rothschild.com/the-house/the-labels-room (Accessed: 20 December 2022).

Christie's (2019) *Art Adorned: Dolce&Gabbana and the Old Masters*, 25 November [YouTube]. Available at: https://www.youtube.com/watch?v=aqJ4hIqd5hA (Accessed: 16 December 2022).

Christie's (2023) *Art Adorned: Christie's × Dolce&Gabbana Alta Gioielleria*. Available at: https://www.christies.com/privatesales/art-adorned-christies-x-dolce-gabbana-alta-gioielleria (Accessed: 5 October 2023).

Clark, A. (2019) "An enquiring mind: Manolo Blahník at the Wallace Collection", *The British Art Journal*, 20/2, p. 87.

Cleary, M. (2021) "Valentino's new Beijing exhibition explores the role of fashion", *Wallpaper*, 18 October. Available at: https://www.wallpaper.com/fashion/valentino-beijing-exhibit-re-signify-part-II (Accessed: 17 May 2022).

Cogley, B. (2019) "Louis Vuitton X celebrates 160 years of artistic collaboration at the fashion house", *Dezeen*, 24 July. Available at: https://www.dezeen.com/2019/07/24/louis-vuitton-x-exhibition-los-angeles/(Accessed: 7 June 2022).

Currid-Halkett, E. (2007) *The Warhol Economy: How Fashion, Art, and Music Drive New York City*. Princeton: Princeton University Press.

Debord, G. (1994) *Society of the Spectacle*. Translated by K. Knabb. London: Rebel Press.

Delanty, G. (2000) *Modernity and Postmodernity: Knowledge, Power and the Self*. London: Sage Publications.

Eckhardt, G.M. and Bardhi, F. (2020) "New dynamics of social status and distinction", *Marketing Theory*, 20/1, pp. 85–102. Available at: https://doi.org/10.1177/1470593119856650.

Elias, N. (1992) *Time: An Essay*. Oxford: Blackwell.

Elliott, M. (2022) "In Washington, DC, Yayoi Kusama and Veuve Clicquot are in full bloom", *Wallpaper*, 13 October. Available at: https://www.wallpaper.com/art/yayoi-kusama-veuve-clicquot-washington-dc#:~:text=in%20full%20bloom-,In%20Washington%2C%20DC%2C%20Yayoi%20Kusama%20and%20Veuve,Clicquot%20are%20in%20full%20bloom&text=It%20was%202006%20when%20Japanese,with%20her%20iconic%20polka%20dots (Accessed: 20 November 2022).

Fabris, G. (2003) *Il nuovo consumatore: verso il postmoderno*. Milano: Franco Angeli.

Firat, A.F. and Venkatesh, A. (1995) "Liberatory postmodernism and the reenchantment of consumption", *Journal of Consumer Research*, 22/3, pp. 239–267. Available at: https://doi.org/10.1086/209448.

Hassan, R. (2009) *Empires of Speed: Time and the Acceleration of Politics and Society*. Leiden: Brill.

Hawkins, L. (2022a) "Yves Saint Laurent takes over six museums in Paris", *Wallpaper*, 6 October. Available at: https://www.wallpaper.com/fashion/-yves-saint-laurent-six-museums-paris-60th-anniversary (Accessed: 21 December 2022).

Hawkins, L. (2022b) "Louis Vuitton × Fornasetti bags are modern treasures", *Wallpaper*, 28 October. Available at: https://www.wallpaper.com/fashion/louis-vuitton-x-fornasetti-bags (Accessed: 15 December 2022).

Joy, A., LaTour, K., Charters, S.J., Grohmann, B. and Peña-Moreno, C. (2021) "The artification of wine: lessons from the fine wines of Bordeaux and Burgundy", *Arts and the Market*, 11/1, pp. 24–39. Available at: https://doi.org/10.1108/AAM-11-2020-0048.

Koons, J. (2017) "The history of art according to Jeff Koons", *Harper's Bazaar*, 12 October. Available at: https://www.harpersbazaar.com/culture/art-books-music/a12823707/jeff-koons-art-history/ (Accessed: 7 March 2022).

Law, J. (2021) "How Jimmy Choo outshines competition with 'Chasing Stars' collaboration", *Jing Daily*, 19 October. Available at: https://jingdaily.com/jimmy-choo-eric-haze-nft-bearbrick-collaboration/ (Accessed: 20 November 2022).

Louis Vuitton (2021) *Women's Fall-Winter 2021 Fashion Show*, 5 March. Available at: https://uk.louisvuitton.com/eng-gb/magazine/articles/women-fall-winter-2021-show-paris# (Accessed: 15 December 2022).

Madden, A. (2021) "Louis Vuitton brings Greek sculptures and Fornasetti prints into 2021", *TZR*, 10 March. Available at: https://www.thezoereport.com/fashion/louis-vuitton-fall-winter-2021-runway-collection (Accessed: 15 December 2022).

Makris, C. (2022) "Perfect Blend", *Apollo*, 1 July, p. 53.

Martineau, J. (2016) *Time, Capitalism and Alienation: A Socio-Historical Inquiry into the Making of Modern Time*. Chicago: Haymarket Books.

Mun-Delsalle, Y.J. (2020a) "French artists Maya Mouawad and Cyril Laurier create technology-driven artworks championing sustainability", *Forbes*, 19 February. Available at: https://www.forbes.com/sites/yjeanmundelsalle/2020/02/19/french-artists-maya-mouawad-and-cyril-laurier-create-technology-driven-artworks-championing-sustaina bility/?sh=4268ca7e66d6 (Accessed: 27 December 2022).

Mun-Delsalle, Y.J. (2020b) "Q&A with Frederic Dufour, President and CEO of Ruinart", *Forbes*, 4 June. Available at: https://www.forbes.com/sites/yjeanmundelsalle/2020/06/04/qa-with-frederic-dufour-president-and-ceo-of-ruinart/?sh=1830bcea56e9 (Accessed: 16 October 2022).

Osborne, P. (1995) *The Politics of Time: Modernity and Avant-Garde*. London: Verso Books.

Palumbo, J. (2019) "Dalí, Hockney, and Koons have all designed labels for this French winery", *Artsy*, 15 March. Available at: https://www.artsy.net/article/artsy-editorial-dali-hockney-koons-designed-labels-french-winery (Accessed 20 December 2021).

Parguel, B., Delécolle, T. and Mimouni Chaabane, A. (2020) "Does fashionization impede luxury brands' CSR image?", *Sustainability*, 12/1, 428, pp. 1–16. https://doi.org/10.3390/su12010428.

Parsons, E. (2019) "Jonathan Anderson fills Ruinart's one-bedroom hotel with designs from his own home", *Wallpaper*, 5 July. Available at: https://www.wallpaper.com/lifestyle/jonathan-anderson-designs-ruinart-1729-hotel-london (Accessed 20 November 2022).

Passariello, C. (2006) "Louis Vuitton tries modern methods on factory lines", *The Wall Street Journal*, 9 October. Available at: https://www.wsj.com/articles/SB116035785257486463 (Accessed 6 November 2022).

Perry, G. (2016) *Playing the Gallery: Helping Contemporary Art in its Struggle to Be Understood*. London: Penguin Books.

Petras, A. (2019) "At a new exhibition, Louis Vuitton's artistic collaborations are front and center", *Galerie*, 28 June. Available at: https://www.galeriemagazine.com/louis-vuitton-opens-louis-vuitton-x-an-immersive-exhibition-of-their-artistic-collaborations/ (Accessed: 20 December 2020).

Phelan, B. (2019) "Bottega Veneta celebrate new Miami store opening with Bottega diner party", *Pause*, 6 December. Available at: https://pausemag.co.uk/2019/12/bottega-veneta-celebrate-new-miami-store-opening-with-bottega-diner-party/ (Accessed: 25 November 2022).

Pine, B.J. II and Gilmore, J.H. (2019) *The Experience Economy: Competing for Customer Time, Attention, and Money*. Boston: Harvard Business Review Press.

Portee, A. (2021) "Dior unveils twelve artists' Dior Lady Art handbags for their sixth edition", *Forbes*, 21 December. Available at: https://www.forbes.com/sites/allysonportee/2021/12/21/dior-unveils-twelve-artists-dior-lady-art-handbags-for-their-sixth-edition/?sh=164f67fe2ef7 (Accessed:20 December 2022).

Prada (2012) *24h Museum*. Available at: https://www.prada.com/gb/en/pradasphere/events/2012/24h-museum.html (Accessed 20 November 2022).

Quinones, R.J. (1972) *The Renaissance Discovery of Time*. Cambridge: Harvard University Press.

Ruinart (2019) *Ruinart × Retour aux Sources*, 30 September [YouTube]. Available at: https://www.youtube.com/watch?v=iWuRcDdOkkA (Accessed: 27 December 2022).

Ruinart (2022a) *Ruinart and Art*. Available at: https://www.ruinart.com/en-us/art/ruinart-and-art (Accessed: 23 December 2022).

Ruinart (2022b) *Ruinart × Mouawad Laurier*. Available at: https://www.ruinart.com/en-gb/mouawadlaurier.html (Accessed: 23 December 2022).

Ruinart (2023) *Alexandre Benjamin Navet*. Available at: https://www.ruinart.com/en-gb/alexandrebenjaminnavet.html (Accessed: 8 October 2023).

Salais, R. and Storper, M. (1992) "The four 'worlds' of contemporary industry", *Cambridge Journal of Economics*, 16/2, pp. 169–193. Available at: https://www.jstor.org/stable/23599540.

Schumacher, E.F. (2011) *Small is Beautiful: A Study of Economics as if People Mattered*. London: Vintage Books.

Sennett, R. (2009) *The Craftsman*. London: Penguin Books.

Serafin, A. (2022) "Past meets present: inside 30 Avenue Montaigne, Dior's new look Parisian flagship", *Wallpaper*, 19 August. Available at: https://www.wallpaper.com/fashion/dior-30-avenue-montaigne-paris-store-museum?utm_source=Selligent&utm_medium=email&utm_campaign=20220407_XWP-X_NWL_EO_Daily-Digest&utm_content=20220407_XWP-X_NWL_EO_Daily-Digest&utm_term=8793155&m_i=FCwv6UGZZcoKIL7ruSixKRMRGL51518dYlE%2BiFGPNfQyDpt0c1mfkOEbt5gzlwFkSBAtWonbE7VQEBZ9BEHVRNhsGrZvNSaFFE&lrh=3d8c79b3364f9758b36d74eaccf9b416214d8f3fb4e6a092d9684146bfdeb5c3&M_BT=38661145981656 (Accessed: 23 August 2022).

Simpson, L.C. (1995) *Technology, Time, and the Conversations of Modernity*. New York: Routledge.

Socha, M. (2021a) "Nicolas Ghesquière takes on mythology, Fornasetti in latest Vuitton collection", *WWD*, 10 March. Available at: https://wwd.com/fashion-news/designer-luxury/exclusive-nicolas-ghesquiere-takes-on-mythology-fornasetti-in-latest-vuitton-collection-1234770866/ (Accessed: 15 December 2022).

Socha, M. (2021b) "Louis Vuitton is celebrating its founder's 200th birthday in a big way", *WWD*, 29 July. Available at: https://wwd.com/fashion-news/designer-luxury/louis-vuitton-200-bicentennial-celebration-1234889762/ (Accessed: 22 December 2022).

Sombart, W. (1967) *Luxury and Capitalism*. Translated by W. R. Dittmar. Ann Arbor: The University of Michigan Press.

Taplin, J. (2017) *Move Fast and Break Things: How Facebook, Google and Amazon Have Cornered Culture and What it Means for All of Us*. London: Macmillan.

Theodosi, N. (2021) "Inside Bottega Veneta's new Shoreditch pop-up", *WWD*, 8 November. Available at: https://wwd.com/fashion-news/fashion-scoops/inside-bottega-venetas-new-shoreditch-pop-up-1234992326/ (Accessed 25 November 2022).

Thomas, D. (2015) *Gods and Kings: The Rise and Fall of Alexander McQueen and John Galliano*. London: Allen Lane.

Thompson, E.P. (1967) "Time, work-discipline, and industrial capitalism", *Past & Present*, 38/1, pp. 56–97. Available at: https://doi.org/10.1093/past/38.1.56.

Valentino (2023a) *Valentino: Re-Signify Part One Shanghai*. Available at: https://www.valentino.com/en-us/experience/valentino-resignify-shanghai (Accessed: 15 January 2023).

Valentino (2023b) *Re-Signify: The Second Chapter*. Available at: https://www.valentino.com/en-cy/experience/valentino-resignify-beijing#:~:text=Risgnification%20 is%20Pierpaolo%20Piccioli's%20personal,but%20with%20an%20emotional%20 involvement (Accessed: 15 January 2023).

Van de Peer, A. (2014) "So last season: the production of the fashion present in the politics of time", *Fashion Theory*, 18/3, pp. 317–339. Available at: https://doi.org/10.2752/175174114X13938552557880.

Vogue (2013) *Damien Hirst × Alexander McQueen by Sølve Sundsbø*, 13 November. Available at: https://www.vogue.com/video/watch/damien-hirst-x-alexander-mcqueen-by-solve-sundsbo (Accessed: 17 January 2023).

Wallace Collection (2019) *An Enquiring Mind: Manolo Blahník at the Wallace Collection*. Available at: https://www.wallacecollection.org/art/exhibitions-displays/past-exhibitions/enquiring-mind-manolo-blahnik-wallace-collection/ (Accessed: 9 January 2023).

Weber, M. (2005) *The Protestant Ethic and the Spirit of Capitalism*. Translated by T. Parsons. London: Routledge. Available at: https://doi.org/10.4324/9780203995808.

Whitrow, G. J. (1988) *Time in History: The Evolution of Our General Awareness of Time and Temporal Perspective*. Oxford: Oxford University Press.

WWD Staff (2015) "Overheated! Is fashion heading for a burnout?", *WWD*, 27 October. Available at: http://wwd.com/fashion-news/fashion-features/fashion-designers-karl-lagerfeldmarc-jacobs-10269092/(Accessed: 24 November 2022).

Zargani, L. (2020) "Pierpaolo Piccioli on Valentino signs, Shanghai brand experience", *WWD*, 18 December. Available at: https://wwd.com/eye/people/pierpaolo-piccioli-on-valentino-signs-shanghai-brand-experience-1234681973/ (Accessed: 15 January 2023).

4 Status and distinction

Objects are characterised by their material finitude and unlimited symbolic capacity. Whilst presenting distinctive appearance and attributes, an object is devoid of any intrinsic value or predetermined meaning: rather, its semantic presence is purely "relational" (Rocamora, 2016, p. 234) and emerges from the ways people make use of it in certain social settings (Bourdieu, 1984; Baudrillard, 2017). From this perspective, consumption is the playfield of "human thought in action" (Lévi-Strauss, 1964, p. 91),[1] where through objects individuals and groups negotiate their identities, enact relations of affiliation and exclusion, shape culture (Douglas and Isherwood, 2021).

Luxury items and works of art are typically associated with and reflective of dynamics of class and prestige. In traditional societies characterised by an ascribed hierarchical system and an upward distribution of wealth and power, conspicuous consumption tends to be an exclusive prerogative of the ruling élites (Mason, 1981): for example, in Renaissance Europe (14th–17th centuries) royal houses, the aristocracy, religious eminences and notable bankers accumulated majestic art pieces and exquisite furnishings, marking their political and social hegemony through a sumptuous lifestyle where even the items fulfilling the most mundane needs would be of the utmost refinement, such as silver graters or urinals of crystal (Hollingsworth, 1994; Guerzoni, 2011).

Over time, an increased socio-political mobility driven by a diversified subdivision of the economic surplus would provide larger groups of the population with a discretionary income for hedonistic purchases. Almost coincidently, the development of a capitalistic mode of production in the 18th and 19th centuries democratised the splendid items of the upper classes releasing on the market their affordable versions: such is the case of the Paisley's shawl, the industrial alternative to the one-of-a-kind, priceless Kashmir stole (Leavitt, 1972) and the square canvas paintings, whose standardised formats efficiently catered the middle-class' burgeoning demand for smaller domestic art (Falcinelli, 2020). In addition, the diffusion of commercial and cultural venues such as department stores and theatres turned the city space into a "dwelling place of the collective" (Benjamin, 1999, p. 879), where the urban

DOI: 10.4324/9781003274094-5

community could indulge in the contemplation of fine items magnificently displayed in the windows of the arcades, in the museums' cabinets, at expositions. The visual appreciation of objects thus became a form of consumption in its own right, further introducing ordinary people to the aesthetics and the imagery of extraordinary goods.[2]

More than just a "special class of things", high-end items should be rather considered a "special 'register' of consumption" (Appadurai, 1986, p. 38), for they also entail a complex acquisition process and specific competences about their proper use. In this regard, it is usually the affiliation to certain social circles that provides their members with the intelligence, connoisseurship and etiquette connoting the acquisition and use of certain goods as status-appropriate or tasteful (Bourdieu, 1984; Douglas and Isherwood, 2021). Pouring milk last when serving tea was the Victorian signifier of one's high standing as it suggested their acquaintance with the finest, heat-proof China cups (Currid-Halkett, 2017). For a long time, the possession of art and its correct appreciation pointed to the wasteful abundance of leisure time and economic resources invested in a subject without any utilitarian application, together with a remarkable social capital accrued through the privileged interaction with critics, gallerists and dealers (Bourdieu, 1984; Veblen, 2007; Stankovic, Tonner and Wilson, 2016).

As previously mentioned, the time-space compression prompted by globalisation and digitalisation has exponentially intensified the circulation of people, goods and information human beings are exposed to. This has gradually eroded long-established social hierarchies generating a "cultural disorder" (Featherstone, 1990, p. 6) also in the objects and practices conventionally regarded as markers of distinction.

Confronted with the overflow of objects, contents and images and their increasing semantic vagueness, the socioeconomic and cultural élites of today – inclusive of digital expats and the urban creative class – have turned to more nuanced ways to signal their position (Chan and Goldthorpe, 2010; Eckhardt and Bardhi, 2020), from intangible activities informed by subtle cultural codes (Currid-Halkett, 2017) to seemingly unassuming consumption modes like minimalism, "another class-dependent way of feeling better about yourself by buying a product, as Spartan as the product might be. It takes a lot of money to look this simple" (Chayka, 2020, p. 39).

Intelligence reports (Highsnobiety and BCG, 2020) indicate that by 2026 millennials and Gen Zers will account for 60 per cent of the global luxury market, with a consolidated relevance of the Asian segments (Tian and Dong, 2010; D'Arpizio et al., 2023). The evolving geography and demographics of luxury consumers add further semantic layers to status consumption. In post-opening China (1978 onwards), the possession of Western prestige goods indicated at first "the middle class's newly acquired socioeconomic status and lifestyles" (Wang, 2014, p. 8), with the first-world provenance of the items providing a further undertone of worldly sophistication. Today's young affluent

Chinese seem less concerned about showing off class and wealth and, as their peers worldwide, seek internationally acclaimed prestige goods – artworks, branded items, collectibles such as sneakers, etc. – to convey their knowledge and cultural fluency (Bargeron, 2022). Inverting the terms of the equation by which consumers' choices stem from their cultural capital, cultural capital is now being commodified as the ultimate status acquisition.

Luxury brand and art collaborations circulate in such a marketplace as a miscellanea of products – material, immaterial, experiential, mediatic – with their own register of consumption. By activating specific dynamics of acquisition and access, collaborations mix extant signals of prestige with emerging status symbols, eventually articulating the postmodern vocabulary of distinction.

Subversive, omnivorous, playful: The new facets of distinction

In outlining the rationale behind the significant diffusion of luxury brand and art collaborations over the past 30 years, scholars typically maintain that the linkup with art has been for luxury brands a means to reconcile their increased availability on the market by conferring some of their products a note of distinctive rarity against the *masstige* of diffusion lines and affordable merchandise (Chailan, 2018).

Interestingly, the artistic forms luxury brands have oftentimes chosen to associate themselves with have marked anti-establishment traits (Nastasijevic, 2014). In the late 1990s, Louis Vuitton's creative director Marc Jacobs ushered in a season of ground-breaking art partnerships with maverick creatives – graffiti artist Stephen Sprouse, controversial photographer Richard Prince, obsessive pop-minimalist Yayoi Kusama and Neo-Pop pioneer Takashi Murakami (Joy and Belk, 2020). In 2008, right when Jacobs was iterating the 2001 Sprouse collaboration for Louis Vuitton's forthcoming collection, fine spirit brand 1800 Tequila launched the Essential Artists project, commissioning their label design to street artists such as UrbanMedium and Shepard Fairey – authors respectively of viral sticker campaigns "CheTrooper" and "Obey Giant" – and reproducing licenced works by Keith Haring and Jean-Michel Basquiat (Hofmann, 2015). A few years later, cognac house Hennessy tapped into graffiti and iconographic art with a series of limited editions by KAWS, Futura, Os Gêmeos, Ryan McGinness and Shepard Fairey (Hofmann, 2015).

The fact that both 1800 Tequila and Hennessy's unconventional art editions mainly interested their entry-level product line has been interpreted as a strategic move to attract young and aspirational consumer demographics through "the outsider reputation" (Hofmann, 2015) of the artists. The next-generation clientele was also the intended recipient of Hermès' Fall/Winter 2011 Graff by Kongo collection, in partnership with street artist Cyril Kongo

(Lai, 2021). Kongo's input on the hyper-classic scarves of Hermès and most recently on Richard Mille's tourbillon watch for a collector's edition of 30 pieces (Kessler, 2022), however, suggests that unorthodox styles appeal to an older and wealthier clientele as well.

Nonconforming art movements unquestionably set themselves in stark contrast to the aesthetic archetypes of luxury, defined by polished elegance and classic sophistication. Kongo considered the commission by Hermès "an unprecedented bet in the history of the brand", for it attempted to bridge two worlds "at the antipodes" (Cyril Kongo, 2023), namely street art and luxury. In the same way, choosing Sprouse to deface Louis Vuitton's monogram with his gritty signature style was for Jacobs "a rebellious act" (Jacobs, in MarcJacobsInterviews, 2013). In truth, through iconoclastic renditions and defiant interpretations, Jacobs-led series of collaborations ended up blurring the lines between high-brow and low-brow culture, good and bad taste, subverting de facto the conventional imaginary of luxury products (Joy and Belk, 2020).

Far from obliterating the prestige sign-value attached to luxury goods (Mortelmans, 2005), these far-fetched collaborations have introduced luxury consumers to "anti-snob snobbism" (Jacobs, in Yotka, 2021; Andjelic, 2023) as a form of social elevation: the transgressive and unapologetic messages of radical art – generally dismissive of the system and its commercial logics, yet here conveniently attached to products on sale – provide consumers with a liberating sense of authenticity and intellectual coolness that mainstream luxury items lack (Hahl, Zuckerman and Kim, 2017; Joy and Belk, 2020). This seemingly defiant consumption choice, furthermore, conveys their careless superiority to societal conventions and normative judgements, setting them apart from more conforming or insecure customer segments such as the traditionalists and the aspirationals (Bellezza, Gino and Keinan, 2014; Bellezza and Berger, 2020).

The original confrontational edge of many countercultural art movements has in time given way to expressions of unconcerned nihilism. Whilst Murakami's works actualise the vision laid out in his "Super Flat Manifesto" (Murakami, 2000) and actively challenge the hierarchical divide between art and commerce, high-brow and low-brow culture as constructs of Western imperialism (Museum of Contemporary Art of Chicago, 2017; Borggreen, 2018), in KAWS' cartoonish paintings and sculptures there is a complete "disavowal of critical intent" (Smith, 2019): here, flat is not an alternative epistemology of reality but the reality itself, presented as a surface devoid of any transcendental meaning and thus open to interpretation. Presenting his Masters collaboration with Louis Vuitton (Chapter 1), Jeff Koons reduces the engagement with the Old Masters from an intellectual to a mere sensorial level – "for me, what's wonderful about art is the emotional experience" (Koons, in Ellison, 2017). In the same vein, graffiti-style artist Trevor Andrew aka Guccighost thus explains the use of logos in Gucci's Fall/Winter 2016 collection: "a symbol can be so much more powerful than words, unrestricted by language and appealing to our senses on many levels. [...] My symbols are kind of free associative in that they can mean anything to anybody" (Andrew, in Gucci, 2023). In more general terms, this interpretive relativism also characterises the postmodern shift of status consumption "from *habitus* to freedom" (Warde, in Chan and Goldthorpe, 2010, p. 6): whereas in the past societies had legitimate arbiters of taste dictating the must-haves and the criteria of propriety and elevation, nowadays each individual or group is entitled to validate their own life- and consumption styles.

Still, there are status implications in the way one navigates this anarchy of taste: cultivating a purposeful versatility across different cultural genres and categories becomes a badge of intellectual distinction, for it showcases the individual's critical independence and vivaciousness as opposed to the indiscriminate appreciation of everything and anything or the narrow-minded pursuit of monothematic interests (Chan and Goldthorpe, 2010).

With luxury brands increasingly exploring in their art initiatives fresh expressive registers and daring aesthetics, only culturally omnivorous audiences can fully capture and enjoy humorous witticisms and playful hints, such as in the case of the Gucci bag with Guccighost's "REAL" spray-painted on it (Bettridge, 2021) or KAWS' reinterpretation of the emblems of Dior as crossed-out-eyed characters, which was meant to add an element of jocosity to the Maison's Spring/Summer 2019 menswear collection (Christian Dior, 2018).

Enriched ownership, diversified access

In many product-based collaborations the unique aura that art endows on luxury items is reinforced by the limited number of pieces released on the market. Drawing from some previous examples (Chapter 1), The Gallery of each Rolls-Royce Phantom is a "one of one" (Rolls-Royce Motor Cars Pressclub, 2022), bespoke creation; the crumpled bottle cap designed by Frank Gehry for Louis Vuitton's fragrance line Les Extraits has been reinterpreted by Murano glassblowing master Simone Cenedese in a 40-piece special edition (Nichol, 2022); the Macallan's Anecdotes of Ages Collection comprises 335 bottles of Macallan whisky from 1967 and Speyside-themed labels by Sir Peter Blake organised in a two-tiered order of scarcity, with only 13 hand-blown bottles carrying Blake's original collages, and the rest carrying replica label of the 13th bottle (The Editors of Artnews, 2021).

The market value of these artistic limited editions reflects their superior status of rarities: one Les Extraits Murano Art Edition bottle retails at €5,000, tenfold higher than the Gehry version (Nichol, 2022); each of the 100 Veuve Clicquot's La Grande Dame 2012 magnums fitted in the sculptural case by Kusama is priced at $36,000 against the basic limited-edition box, worth $195 (Suhrawardi, 2020).

A few of these pieces understandably reappear on the secondary market. Balloon Venus, the case created by Jeff Koons for Dom Pérignon in 2013 as a limited edition of 650 pieces, is oftentimes listed for sale at auctions: a Balloon Venus bottle offered at Christie's in 2017 fetched £31,250, doubling the original retail price of £15,500 (Fong, 2013; Christie's, 2017). Besides secondary sales, auctions are utilised as launch platforms for artistic collaborations: one of the original 13 Macallan Anecdotes of Ages bottles was sold at Sotheby's for $437,500 (Sotheby's, 2021); Beverly Hirst Recycler, the fashion collection by Damien Hirst and designer Tetsuzo Okubo made of upcycled garments from Hirst's personal wardrobe, was auctioned on Virgil Abloh's digital art shop Canary Yellow, one dropping per day (Shaw, 2021). Whilst the sale of collaborative pieces through a renowned auction house elevates their product status – already special for their embedded artistic features and numbered availability – to that of cult collectibles, the auction format further amplifies their scarcity appeal by imposing specific spatial-temporal limitations to the sale and leaving the hammer price to be set by the bidders' drive to acquire the lot or win (Wolf, Arkes and Muhanna, 2006).

The online environment presents at first the opposite scenario: by allowing the infinite replication and circulation of objects and contents, web technologies somehow challenge the relevance of possession, originality and authorship. The recent appearance of NFTs, digital products characterised by traceability and non-exchangeability, seems to have nonetheless rekindled "our emotional attachment to ownership" (Tang, in Lord, 2021).

Within their art collaborative initiatives, luxury brands have started releasing NFTs and other digital outputs to further valorise the acquisition of physical products: the 100 unisex shirts designed by Prada with spray paint artist Cassius Hirst and dropped on the brand's online-only platform Timecapsule were accompanied by NFTs, including the drop's serial number and further unspecified content (Hirschmiller, 2022; Salibian, 2022). For their third NFT-based artistic partnership in 2022, fashion house Givenchy enlisted Web 3.0 art collective Felt Zine to realise digital twins of six pieces of their streetwear collection, redeemable only upon purchase of the physical wearables (Schulz, 2022). Selfridges integrated NFTs into their in-store experience: from January to March 2022 visitors to the Corner Shop pop-up could get hold of Paco Rabanne's latest collection inspired by the work of Op Art representative Victor Vasarely – also exhibited in the space – and of 1800 NFTs reproducing the collection and other vintage pieces, all with the same credit card (McDowell, 2022a). By admitting traditional payment forms, Selfridges further widened NFTs' circulation beyond the crypto market.

The segmented distribution of NFTs has become an integral part of luxury brands' velvet-rope strategy, allowing them to further segment customers and audiences across the different touchpoints of their collaborative projects. On its 70th anniversary, high-end outerwear brand Moncler launched an NFT campaign with tokens, including artworks by 3D visual artist Antoni Tudisco.

The campaign was activated in three streams, with 500 NFTs gifted to the buyers of the platinum Moncler Maya 70 jacket, another 500 to the first 500 visitors of the travelling exhibition *Extraordinary Expedition* and 70 exclusively awarded to the "friends of the brand" (Ahssen, 2022; Sinclair, 2023). Besides physical products, Jimmy Choo's collaboration with graffiti artist Eric Haze and fashion designer Poggy (Chapter 3) was digitally released on the cryptoasset marketplace Binance: the only NFT featuring the collaboration sneaker was auctioned, while 8,888 mystery boxes were sold at a fixed price of 30 Binance USD (Perper, 2021). Each box contained a random combination of four NFT cards, all reproducing the Jimmy Choo × Eric Haze LOVE 100 Glitter stilettos according to a four-level scale of rarity, from neutral (5,333 cards) to super-super rare (1 card). The drawers of the super-super rare and super-rare cards had the chance to receive a special NFT by Jimmy Choo (Ucollex, 2021).

In like manner, other brands experiment with playful distribution formats: on the app *Louis: the Game* released by Louis Vuitton for the 200th birth anniversary of their founder (Chapter 3), only the players reaching a certain level in the game would qualify for a raffle to win NFTs by celebrity artists like Beeple (Anderrson, 2022); to get hold of Gucci's digital bag, gamers on platform Roblox had, among other tasks, to turn into artists and create 45 artworks (McDowell, 2022b).

In the resulting variety of physical and digital scarcity defining these collaborative outputs, the acquisition of a specific product is thus determined not solely by one's social standing or "hard cash" (Trunzo, DeLeon and Dreesen, 2018, p. 8) but increasingly by their ability to reach a game level, complete a challenge or by sheer luck. This reflects the emergence of new luxury consumption clusters of Web 3.0 natives, gamers, NFT wallets and cryptocurrency holders, as well as the growing relevance of customers and audiences' engagement with luxury brands on multiple platforms in order to unlock specific tokens of distinction – exclusive experiences, limited treats or admission to the brand's inner circle.

The prestige value and cultural nuances of experience

The recent revival of ownership inserts itself in a landscape that has been largely dominated by experiential consumption (Bardhi and Eckhardt, 2017): visitors to an exhibition purchase admission without having to purchase the pieces on display (Chen, 2009); attending a couture fashion show becomes "a shared, vicarious experience [...] where simply being able to appreciate is enough" (Campbell, 2021); the events and side initiatives of art fairs such as Frieze and Art Basel generate a "collective spiritual state" (Mauss, in Schultheis et al., 2015, p. 134) that is equally shared by art buyers and mere attendees.

Set against material possessions, experiences are deemed to hold a greater degree of uniqueness and irreducibility to comparison in monetary terms, for they emerge from the personal engagement of individuals with objects through context-specific stimuli – cognitive, sensorial and emotional – which they will recall in memories or in their accounts to others (Gilovich, Kumar and Jampol, 2015; Pine and Gilmore, 2019). It is specifically the distinctive "story value" (Gilovich et al., 2015, p. 156) of these events that people can leverage in social settings as "'decontextuali[s]ed' cultural capital" (Weinberger et al., in Eckhardt and Bardhi, 2020, p. 94) to enhance their sense of self and social esteem.

As detailed in previous chapters, luxury brands have integrated art into retail design to magnify the experiential cachet of their customer journey and into museum exhibitions to dramatise their heritage. Depending on the format chosen, these art-enhanced, immaterial propositions enable luxury brands to engage a broader audience than the buying clientele: store window activations – see the performance of Daphne Guinness at Barneys (Chapter 2) or Kusama's takeover in the most recent collaboration with Louis Vuitton (Parkes, 2023) – transfigure and enliven the passersby's interaction with the urban surroundings; the staircase of Dior's first in-house fashion shows (Chapter 2) is a brand historical attraction that can be enjoyed not only by the clients of the Parisian flagship store but also by regular visitors of the contiguous La Galerie Dior on guided tours (Serafin, 2022).

In fact, the luxury brands' portfolio of experiential offerings typically articulates across different levels of accessibility and engagement. Exclusive to their Chinese clientele, in 2017 Hermès organised with graphic designer Jean-Paul Goude the Hermès Club, a one-night-only event in Shanghai where 1000 selected guests dined, enjoyed flamenco shows, played billiards and Mikado in dramatic settings that artfully reinterpreted the iconic products and stylistic codes of the Maison (Pithers, 2017). At the opposite end, Hermès invited the general public to a behind-the-scenes tour of its manufacturing process: during the "*Hors-Champ* (Off-camera)" exhibition at the Shanghai Power Station of Art in 2021, the work of the *petites mains* (craftspeople) was staged as a live interactive performance, where artisans took the attendees through the secrets of *maroquinerie* (leather craft) (Weiyun, 2021).

Similarly to material objects, access-based outputs have in years achieved a spectacular complexity, bundling together educational, entertaining and aesthetic cues to capture the audience's attention. "Make Your Own Path" was designed by Cartier in 2020 to engage Chinese millennials and Gen Zers in a series of interconnected attractions: the display at Shanghai's landmarks of eight artworks commissioned to young Chinese artists; a related exhibition at the Power Station of Art, which also introduced the new Pasha De Cartier watches; a livestreamed clubbing event linked to a 1.1-billion-view Douyin campaign inviting users to share their dance moves (Jing Daily, 2022). Feeding into the fear-of-missing-out (FOMO) culture of today, such collective events with extreme space-temporal restrictions sublimate the prestige value of experience into cultural currency, whereby being *in the know and in the now* refers to the privileged condition of the individual to be part of luxury brands' cultural scene (Atwal, 2021).

New generations of Chinese consumers appear particularly receptive to experiential consumption, enjoying time in retail cafés, pop-up stores or museum exhibitions as well as participating in more immersive activities like treasure hunts and action role plays (Williams, 2021; Jing Daily, 2022). In 2009 Chinese retail billionaire Adrian Cheng launched the K-11 Art Mall, hosting luxury boutiques together with residencies for local artists and blockbuster exhibitions with Western high-calibre cultural institutions, including the Centre Pompidou and the Royal Academy of Arts (Laurent, 2019). Opened first in Hong Kong and subsequently in other locations including Shanghai, Wuhan and Guangzhou, K-11 has introduced a novel experiential format: the "museum-retail" or "curetail" (Wu, 2020).

From a Western perspective the Chinese interaction with foreign cultural and material goods after the country's economic liberalisation has been characterised by "extreme secularism" (Jaffrelot and van der Veer, 2008, p. 25), with artworks introduced in purely commercial settings as culture with a price tag, and European cultural tours blending museum visits and other sightseeing activities with luxury shopping (Ho, 2008; Rovai, 2016). However, as Cheng stresses, the separation between aesthetic appreciation and material consumption is an alien concept in Chinese culture: "walking into a 'white cube' is not only intimidating; it is a foreign experience based on a concept that has not been ingrained in the psyches of most Chinese" (Cheng, in Adam, 2016).

Somehow akin to Murakami's "Super Flat Manifesto", with K-11 Art Mall Cheng challenges Western aesthetics and cultural constructs, legitimising the existence of a Chinese way in the experience of beauty across contemplation and consumption, with a focus on youngsters' practices and habits: "they often consume art much like they consume the 'goods' in the art mall. They take pictures and videos and share them on social media. But at the same time, they are also learning a great deal" (Cheng, in Adam, 2016). Within the globalised experiential ecosystem of luxury and art, local nuances become key activators of interactions that are meaningful, memorable and transformational.

CASE

Old Masters, new customers: The "Victoria Beckham effect" on Sotheby's business evolution

it's the V.B. effect

(Alex Bell [Reyburn, 2018])

At the end of June 2018 Sotheby's auction house and eponymous brand founder Victoria Beckham joined forces in a six-day exhibition of Old Master paintings (Sotheby's, 2018). Held at Beckham's Dover Street store ahead of Sotheby's Old Masters summer sale, the preview exhibition presented a selection of 16 portraits from the lots on auction, which included works by Peter Paul Rubens, Lucas Cranach the Elder and the Circle of Leonardo da Vinci (Finch, 2018). The paintings were hung on the white walls of the boutique among pieces of Beckham's Pre-Fall collection, between windows or arranged in groups together with reflecting geometric fixtures. Artists' quotes about representation and portraiture marked the itinerary of the visit (Gerlis, 2018; Sotheby's, 2018).

The linked auction sale a few days later recorded an encouraging performance for the "notoriously patchy" (Brady, 2018) market of the Old Masters: despite the absence of a blockbuster masterpiece, Sotheby's sold over three quarters of the available lots, securing in total £42.6 million against the lower estimate of £33.1 million (Brady, 2018). Interestingly, a few of the top-seller paintings had appeared in Beckham's exhibition: the 15th-century portrait of Mary of Burgundy and Cranach the Elder's *Portrait of a Man* (c.1508) both sold on or above the upper estimate, while the *Portrait of a Venetian Nobleman* (c.1620) by Rubens – Beckham's personal favourite – was the top-lot, fetching £4.6 million in excluded fees (Brady, 2018). Equally remarkable was the engagement of the public: 7,100 visitors queued for the presale view at Sotheby's, doubling the usual figures, and another 1,250 attended Beckham's in-store exhibition (Brady, 2018). On the social media front, the iconic picture of Victoria Beckham standing next to a Leonardesque portrait of a lady received more than 192,000 Instagram likes (Reyburn, 2018).

Commenting on such an outpouring of attention Sotheby's co-chairman of Old Master paintings Alex Bell coined the catchphrase "Victoria Beckham effect" to acknowledge the positive impact of the collaboration (Reyburn, 2018).

Considerations

Sotheby's partnership with Victoria Beckham was part of a more general attempt by the art sector of the time to revive the appeal of antique artworks by involving media artists and celebrities: in the same year of the Victoria Beckham × Old Master Paintings initiative, the Louvre hosted power couple Jay-Z and Beyoncé to shoot the video *Apes**t* among their iconic masterpieces, which resulted into a record-breaking number of visitors (Chrisafis, 2019); one year earlier, on the occasion of the *Salvator Mundi*'s world tour, Christie's released a YouTube video capturing the visitors' reactions to the painting, which also featured Patti Smith and Leonardo DiCaprio. The video attracted more than 350,000 views (Avery, 2019).

Among the prestige objects in Western culture, Old Masters might be the ones exuding the highest degree of exclusivity: a chronic scarce supply limits their ownership, and their adequate appreciation, as previously mentioned, is closely associated with very specific expert knowledge (Stankovic, Tonner and Wilson, 2016). In a globalised context of consumption where countless cultural, geographical and generational variables intervene to diversify the criteria of distinction and its social indicators, not only are Old Master paintings losing their prominence as status symbols, but the widening temporal gap with younger generations put them at risk of becoming unintelligible, hence culturally obsolete.

Sotheby's collaboration with Victoria Beckham aimed at restoring the Old Masters' salience by reducing the intellectual distance with the current audiences. In the video presentation of the initiative, Beckham shuns away from assuming the role of art curator; rather, she presents herself as "a sponge" (Beckham, in Sotheby's, 2018), an amateur eager to learn. Her self-attributed status of art outsider turns her into an effective interface to relate with ordinary people and normalise their unfamiliarity towards ancient art. Beckham's naïf, unpretentious approach is echoed by then Sotheby's Old Master specialist Chloe Stead, who in turn maintains that the favourite part of her job is "introduc[ing] Old Masters to people who don't know them yet" (Stead, in Sotheby's, 2018). As opposed to Koons' aforementioned emotional approach to the Old Masters, Beckham and Stead promote instead education – albeit glamourised – as the conduit to a deeper, meaningful engagement with the art of the past (Pine and Gilmore, 2019).

In addition, Beckham's in-store exhibition widened the sphere of influence of Old Master paintings from the context of the auction house. Formally open to the public, auction houses' previews are in fact generally perceived to be an exclusive space for art insiders – collectors, traders, market analysists and experts. The choice to organise an exhibition in a retail venue provided an alternative access-based offering, which in turn allowed a more heterogenous visiting base to admire the paintings before possibly entering into private hands. Temporarily liberated from the state of traded collectibles, the selected Old Masters paintings were in turn proposed within an appealing curatorial frame: the theme of self-representation particularly resonated with the contemporary celebrity and social media culture, as epitomised by the persona of Victoria Beckham.

Victoria Beckham × Old Masters Paintings would have a second iteration that same year with "The Female Triumphant", a retail preview of Sotheby's winter Old Master sale focussing on female artists from the 16th through the 19th centuries, and a reception with Frick Young Fellows, where Beckham addressed the issue of youngsters' education on female Old Masters (Sporn, 2019).

The significance of the collaboration had far-reaching implications beyond the reappreciation of historic Western painting. In truth, some critics downplayed Beckham's involvement with Old Masters due to her popstar beginnings as the Posh Spice Girl; however, more than other potential partners with an art pedigree, it was Beckham's *posh* popularity, i.e., her distinctive social capital comprising the glitterati of sport, fashion and showbusiness that opened Sotheby's to look past the niche audience of art connoisseurs.

This also propelled the auction house to enlarge its business focus from the sole trading of high-brow artistic pieces to include objects with a high cultural currency, namely sport memorabilia and branded collectibles, which was formalised as a proper revenue stream with the opening of the luxury and streetwear divisions in 2020 and 2021 (Sporn, 2020; Kennedy, 2023). In so doing, not only was Sotheby's able to lure young buyers to potentially convert them into art collecting at a later stage, but through its reputation in sourcing and authentication, the auction house elevated commercial goods to cultural objects, thus increasing their supply of rarities (Nelson, 2020; Kennedy, 2023).

Through the unusual tie-up between Beckham and the Old Masters, Sotheby's recalibrated the art market between ownership and experience, elitism and popularisation, further consolidating its business transformation at the intersection of contemporary aesthetics and cultural consumption.

Notes

1 In his pivotal essay on tribal totemism, anthropologist Claude Lévi-Strauss posed that a clan would adopt certain animals or artefacts as insignia not for their utilitarian or economic value but because they were "good to think" (Lévi-Strauss, 1964, p. 89), i.e., for their quality to embody that clan's cultural traits and social ties.
2 As for the art appreciation, the bourgeoisie advanced the argument that the onlooker's engagement with an art piece in a museum or at an exhibition is an intellectual activity independent from – and even superior to – its plain possession, thus compensating for the aristocracy's hitherto exclusive access to art through ownership (Wiesing, 2019).

Bibliography

Adam, G. (2016) "Art in shopping malls: it's all product after all", *The Art Newspaper*, 2 February. Available at: https://www.theartnewspaper.com/2016/02/02/art-in-shopping-malls-its-all-product-after-all (Accessed: 23 February 2023).
Ahssen, S. (2022) "Moncler launches its first NFTs", *Fashion Network*, 14 October. Available at: https://ww.fashionnetwork.com/news/Moncler-launches-its-first-nfts, 1448866.html (Accessed: 20 April 2023).
Anderrson, S. (2022) "Louis Vuitton NFT game registers over 2 million downloads", *The Coin Republic*, 3 May. Available at: https://www.thecoinrepublic.com/2022/05/03/louis-vuitton-nft-game-registers-over-2-million-downloads/?utm_source=CryptoNews&utm_medium=app (Accessed: 7 February 2023).
Andjelic, A. (2023) "The Jacobs effect", *The Sociology of Business*, 6 March. Available at: https://andjelicaaa.substack.com/p/the-jacobs-effect (Accessed: 15 March 2023).

Appadurai, A. (1986) "Introduction: commodities and the politics of value", in A. Appadurai (ed.) *The Social Life of Things: Commodities in Cultural Perspective*. Cambridge: Cambridge University Press, pp. 3–63.

Atwal, G. (2021) "5 ways luxury brands can win over the FOMO generation", *Jing Daily*, 12 May. Available at: https://jingdaily.com/fomo-luxury-brands-gen-zers-china/ (Accessed: 15 February 2023).

Avery, J. (2019) "Christie's and Leonardo Da Vinci's Salvator Mundi: the value of a brand", *Harvard Business School* [Ref. 518-006]. Available at: https://www.hbs.edu/faculty/Pages/item.aspx?num=53659.

Bardhi, F. and Eckhardt, G.M. (2017) "Liquid consumption", *Journal of Consumer Research*, 44/3, pp. 582–597. Available at: https://doi.org/10.1093/jcr/ucx050.

Bargeron, S. (2022) "Why Chinese consumers are not your average art collectors", *Jing Daily*, 24 November. Available at: https://jingdaily.com/chinese-cultural-consumer-art-collectors/ (Accessed: 18 February 2023).

Baudrillard, J. (2017) *The Consumer Society: Myths and Structures*. London: Sage Publications.

Bellezza, S. and Berger, J. (2020) "Trickle-round signals: when low status is mixed with high", *Journal of Consumer Research*, 47/1, pp. 100–127. Available at: https://doi.org/10.1093/jcr/ucz049.

Bellezza, S., Gino, F. and Keinan, A. (2014) "The red sneakers effect: inferring status and competence from signals of nonconformity", *Journal of Consumer Research*, 41/1, pp. 35–54. Available at: https://doi.org/10.1086/674870.

Benjamin, W. (1999) *The Arcades Project*. Translated by H. Eiland and K. McLaughlin. Cambridge: The Belknap Press of Harvard University Press.

Bettridge, T. (2021) "Meet the 60 year old can of poop that explains contemporary fashion", *Highsnobiety*, 17 June. Available at: https://www.highsnobiety.com/p/piero-manzoni-artists-shit-fashion-irony/?utm_source=Highsnobiety+Newsletter&utm_campaign=315a5a9921-INSIGHTS_Artists-Shit_June-24&utm_medium=email&utm_term=0_54b284222a-315a5a9921-87232034&mc_cid=315a5a9921&mc_eid=2a296f6214 (Accessed: 14 February 2023).

Borggreen, G. (2018) "Art and consumption in post-bubble Japan: from postmodern irony to shared engagement", in K.J. Cwiertka and E. Machotka (eds.) *Consuming Life in Post-bubble Japan: A Transdisciplinary Perspective*. Amsterdam: Amsterdam University Press, pp. 175–194.

Bourdieu, P. (1984) *Distinction: A Social Critique of the Judgement of Taste*. Translated by R. Nice. Cambridge: Harvard University Press.

Brady, A. (2018) "Guarantees, the Beckham effect and warts-and-all portraits: Sotheby's pulls off a consistent Old Master sale", *The Art Newspaper*, 5 July. Available at: https://www.theartnewspaper.com/2018/07/05/guarantees-the-beckham-effect-and-warts-and-all-portraits-sothebys-pulls-off-a-consistent-old-master-sale (Accessed: 13 April 2023).

Campbell, G. (2021) "Men's couture is a wave, not a gimmick", *Higsnobiety*, 16 July. Available at: https://www.highsnobiety.com/p/mens-couture-review/ (Accessed: 20 April 2023).

Chailan, C. (2018) "Art as a means to recreate luxury brands' rarity and value", *Journal of Business Research*, 85, pp. 414–423. Available at: https://doi.org/10.1016/j.jbusres.2017.10.019.

Chan, T.W. and Goldthorpe, J.H. (2010) "Introduction: social status and cultural consumption", in T.W. Chan (ed.) *Social Status and Cultural Consumption*. Cambridge: Cambridge University Press, pp. 1–27.

Chayka, K. (2020) *The Longing for Less: Living with Minimalism.* New York: Blooms-bury Publishing.

Chen, Y. (2009) "Possession and access: consumer desires and value perceptions re-garding contemporary art collection and exhibit visits", *Journal of Consumer Re-search*, 35/6, pp. 925–940. Available at: http://dx.doi.org/10.1086/593699.

Chrisafis, A. (2019) "Beyoncé and Jay-Z help Louvre museum break visitor record in 2018", *The Guardian*, 3 January. Available at: https://www.theguardian.com/world/2019/jan/03/beyonce-jay-z-help-louvre-museum-break-visitor-record (Accessed: 19 April 2023).

Christian Dior (2018) *Dior Men's Summer 2019 Show: Interview with KAWS*, 27 June [YouTube]. Available at: https://www.youtube.com/watch?v=M-bK6I8oQxc (Ac-cessed: 12 March 2023).

Christie's (2017) *Dom Pérignon Balloon Venus.* Available at: https://www.christies.com/en/lot/lot-6062314 (Accessed: 20 March 2023).

Currid-Halkett, E. (2017) *The Sum of Small Things: A Theory of the Aspirational Class.* Princeton: Princeton University Press.

Cyril Kongo (2023) *Hermès.* Available at: https://cyrilkongo.art/dialogues/hermes/ (Accessed: 12 March 2023).

D'Arpizio, C., Levato, F., Prete, F. and de Montgolfier, J. (2023) "Renaissance in uncertainty: luxury builds on its rebound", *Bain & Company*, 17 January. Avail-able at: https://www.bain.com/insights/renaissance-in-uncertainty-luxury-builds-on-its-rebound/#:~:text=The%20luxury%20market's%20consumer%20base,compared%20with%2035%25%20last%20year (Accessed: 18 February 2023).

Douglas, M. and Isherwood, B. (2021) *The World of Goods.* New York: Routledge.

Eckhardt, G.M. and Bardhi, F. (2020) "New dynamics of social status and dis-tinction", *Marketing Theory*, 20/1, pp. 85–102. Available at: https://doi.org/10.1177/1470593119856650.

Ellison, J. (2017) "Master pieces? Jeff Koons on his first collaboration with Louis Vuit-ton", *Financial Times*, 11 April. Available at: https://www.ft.com/content/354c71d0-1dfe-11e7-b7d3-163f5a7f229c (Accessed: 10 March 2022).

Estiler, K. (2020) 'Yayoi Kusama's famous polka dots adorn Veuve Clicquot champagne collaboration', *Hypebeast*, 9 September. Available at: https://hypebeast.com/2020/9/yayoi-kusama-veuve-clicquot-champagne-collaboration-info (Accessed: 13 February 2013).

Falcinelli, R. (2020) *Figure: come funzionano le immagini dal Rinascimento a Insta-gram.* Torino: Einaudi.

Featherstone, M. (1990) "Perspectives on consumer culture", *Sociology*, 24/1, pp. 5–22.

Finch, M. (2018) "Victoria Beckham: modern muse among the Masters", *Sotheby's*, 22 June. Available at: https://www.sothebys.com/en/articles/victoria-beckham-modern-muse-among-the-masters (Accessed: 16 April 2023).

Fong, A. (2013) "Jeff Koons for Dom Pérignon collaboration", *Glass*, 4 November. Avail-able at: https://www.theglassmagazine.com/jeff-koons-for-dom-perignon-collaboration/ (Accessed: 2 April 2023).

Gerlis, M. (2018) "Master influencer: Victoria Beckham shows Old Masters", *Finan-cial Times*, 22 June. Available at: https://www.ft.com/content/896171c6-746a-11e8-bab2-43bd4ae655dd (Accessed: 8 May 2023).

Gilovich, T., Kumar, A. and Jampol, L. (2015) "A wonderful life: experiential consump-tion and the pursuit of happiness", *Journal of Consumer Psychology*, 25/1, pp.152–165. Available at: http://dx.doi.org/10.1016/j.jcps.2014.08.004.

Gucci (2023) *Chatting with Trouble Andrew*. Available at: https://www.gucci.com/us/en/st/stories/inspirations-and-codes/article/agenda_2016_issue05_guccighost_collection_trouble_andrew_qa (Accessed: 12 March 2023).

Guerzoni, G. (2011) *Apollo and Vulcan: The Art Markets in Italy, 1400–1700*. East Lansing: Michigan State University Press.

Hahl, O., Zuckerman, E.W. and Kim, M. (2017) "Why elites love authentic lowbrow culture: overcoming high-status denigration with outsider art", *American Sociological Review*, 82/4, pp. 828–856. Available at: https://doi.org/10.1177/0003122417710642.

Highsnobiety and BCG (2020) *Culture Culture Culture*. Available at: https://static.highsnobiety.com/assets/documents/HighsnobietyxBCG_-_Culture_Culture_Culture.pdf (Accessed: 18 February 2023).

Hirschmiller, S. (2022) "The disruptive idea behind Prada's new Timecapsule NFT collection with Damien Hirst's son", *Forbes*, 30 May. Available at: https://www.forbes.com/sites/stephaniehirschmiller/2022/05/30/prada-launches-timecapsule-nft-collection-with-cass-hirst/ (Accessed: 8 May 2023).

Ho, P. (2008) "Consuming art in middle class China", in C. Jaffrelot and P. van der Veer (eds.) *Patterns of Middle Class Consumption in India and China*. Los Angeles: Sage Publications, pp. 277–291.

Hofmann, R. (2015) "Strange bedfellows: the new mashup of big booze and street art", *Punch*, 29 September. Available at: https://punchdrink.com/articles/the-new-mashup-of-spirits-brands-and-artists-1800-tequila-keith-haring-absolut-warhol/ (Accessed: 27 February 2022).

Hollingsworth, M. (1994) *Patronage in Renaissance Italy: from 1400 to the Early Sixteenth Century*. Baltimore: Johns Hopkins University Press.

Jaffrelot, C. and van der Veer, P. (2008) "Introduction", in C. Jaffrelot and P. van der Veer (eds.) *Patterns of Middle Class Consumption in India and China*. Los Angeles: Sage Publications, pp. 11–34.

Jing Daily (2022) "When it comes to hard luxury, China's digital natives want real-life experiences", *Jing Daily*, 8 August. Available at: https://jingdaily.com/hard-luxury-gen-z-china-pop-up/ (Accessed: 14 February 2023).

Joy, A. and Belk, R.W. (2020) "Why luxury brands partner with artists", in P.Y. Donzé, V. Pouillard and J. Roberts (eds.) *The Oxford Handbook of Luxury Business*. New York: Oxford University Press, pp. 309–329.

Kennedy, J. (2023) "Fashion's future at auction houses", *Business of Fashion*, 20 March. Available at: https://www.businessoffashion.com/articles/luxury/fashions-future-at-auction-houses/?utm_source=newsletter_dailydigest&utm_medium=email&utm_campaign=Daily_Digest_200323&utm_content=intro (Accessed: 21 March 2023).

Kessler, K. (2022) "Playing tag: Kongo's riot of colour for Richard Mille", *Wallpaper*, 9 August. Available at: https://www.wallpaper.com/watches-and-jewellery/street-artist-kongo-designs-watch-for-richard-mille (Accessed: 3 March 2023).

Lai, K. (2021) "Graffiti artist Cyril Kongo on designing for Hermès and the luxury world", *#legend*, 26 February. Available at: https://hashtaglegend.com/magazine/graffiti-artist-cyril-kongo-hermes-luxury/ (Accessed: 12 March 2023).

Laurent, T. (2019) "How art saves the malls – lessons from China", *Jing Daily*, 30 June. Available at: https://jingdaily.com/art-malls-lessons-china/ (Accessed: 23 February 2023).

Leavitt, T.W. (1972) "Fashion, commerce and technology in the nineteenth century: the shawl trade", *Textile History*, 3/1, pp. 51–63. Available at: https://doi. org/10.1179/004049672793692228.

Lévi-Strauss, C. (1964) *Totemism*. Translated by R. Needham. London: Merlin Press.

Lord, R. (2021) "Why Gucci and Rimowa are cashing in with NFTs – after the digital art boom, luxury brands are next to ride the crypto wave", *Style*, 26 July. Available at: https://www.scmp.com/magazines/style/news-trends/article/3142511/why-gucci-and-rimowa-are-cashing-nfts-after-digital-art (Accessed: 14 February 2023).

MarcJacobsInterviews (2013) *Marc Jacobs on Stephen Sprouse for Louis Vuitton*, 3 March [YouTube]. Available at: https://www.youtube.com/watch?v=bNnX63RZn3g (Accessed: 12 March 2023).

Mason, R.S. (1981) *Conspicuous Consumption: A Study of Exceptional Consumer Behavior*. New York: St. Martin's Press.

McDowell, M. (2022a) "Selfridges is selling NFTs in store", *Vogue Business*, 13 January. Available at: https://www.voguebusiness.com/technology/selfridges-is-selling-nfts-in-store (Accessed: 20 March 2023).

McDowell, M. (2022b) "When it comes to Roblox, Gucci is not playing around", *Vogue Business*, 27 May. Available at: https://www.voguebusiness.com/technology/when-it-comes-to-roblox-gucci-is-not-playing-around?uID=50002d73c8fdbd69cda a7c14bd0722df05f006fce4e038b332fbb7c8861b9e9a&utm_campaign=newsletter_ weekly&utm_source=newsletter&utm_brand=vb&utm_mailing=VB_NEWS_ MONDAY_300522&utm_medium=email&utm_term=VB_VogueBusiness (Accessed: 8 May 2023).

Mortelmans, D. (2005) "Sign values in processes of distinction: the concept of luxury", *Semiotica*, 157, pp. 497–520. Available at: https://doi.org/10.1515/ semi.2005.2005.157.1-4.497.

Murakami, T. (2000) *Superflat*. Tokyo: Madra Publishing.

Museum of Contemporary Art of Chicago (2017) *Takashi Murakami*, 9 June [YouTube]. Available at: https://www.youtube.com/watch?v=-YPOWBQAd1M (Accessed: 12 March 2023).

Nastasijevic, A. (2014) "10 street art fashion collaborations", *Widewalls*, 2 June. Available at: https://www.widewalls.ch/magazine/10-fashion-collaborations/kaws-x-pharrell-x-comme-de-garcons (Accessed: 8 May 2023).

Nelson, T. (2020) "Sotheby's to auction rare artist-designed Nike sneakers", *Architectural Digest*, 23 September. Available at: https://www.architecturaldigest.com/ story/sothebys-auction-rare-artist-designed-nike-sneakers (Accessed: 13 February 2023).

Nichol, K. (2022) "Louis Vuitton's Les Extraits Murano Art Edition honors Venetian glassmaking", *Formes De Luxe*, 21 October. Available at: https://www.formesde-luxe.com/article/fragrance-becomes-art-with-louis-vuitton-s-les-extraits-murano-art-edition.61577 (Accessed: 18 March 2023).

Parkes, J. (2023) "Louis Vuitton overhauls stores with Yayoi Kusama polka-dots and life-like animatronics", *Dezeen*, 15 January. Available at: https://www.dezeen. com/2023/01/15/louis-vuitton-yayoi-kusama-polkadots-stores/ (Accessed: 11 April 2023).

Perper, R. (2021) "Jimmy Choo teams up with Eric Haze and Poggy for limited-edition NFT", *Hypebeast*, 15 October. Available at: https://hypebeast.com/2021/10/jimmy-choo-eric-haze-nft-binance (Accessed: 15 February 2023).

Pine, B.J. II and Gilmore, J.H. (2019) *The Experience Economy: Competing for Customer Time, Attention, and Money*. Boston: Harvard Business Review Press.

Pithers, E. (2017) "Exclusive: inside Shanghai's Hermès Club", *British Vogue*, 20 June. Available at: https://www.vogue.co.uk/article/hermes-shanghai-emerging-market-china-exclusive-event (Accessed: 6 May 2023).

Reyburn, S. (2018) "Celebrities love old masters, but will collectors fall for them?", *New York Times*, 6 July. Available at: https://www.nytimes.com/2018/07/06/arts/design/art-collectors-old-masters.html (Accessed: 7 February 2023).

Rocamora, A. (2016) "Pierre Bourdieu: the field of fashion", in A. Rocamora and A. Smelik (eds.) *Thinking Through Fashion: A Guide to Key Theorists*. London: I.B. Tauris, pp. 233–250.

Rolls-Royce Motor Cars Pressclub (2022) *Phantom Orchid an inspirational symbol for our times*. Available at: https://www.press.rolls-roycemotorcars.com/rolls-royce-motor-cars-pressclub/article/detail/T0365954EN/phantom-orchid-an-inspirational-symbol-for-our-times (Accessed: 27 February 2022).

Rovai, S. (2016) *Luxury the Chinese Way: New Competitive Scenarios*. Basingstoke: Palgrave Macmillan.

Salibian, S. (2022) "Prada adds NFTs to Timecapsule project", *WWD*, 30 May. Available at: https://wwd.com/fashion-news/fashion-scoops/prada-nfts-timecapsule-project-discord-1235191452/ (Accessed: 25 April 2023).

Schultheis, F., Single, E., Egger, S. and Mazzurana, T. (2015) *When Art Meets Money: Encounters at the Art Basel*. Translated by J. Fearns. Köln: Verlag der Buchhandlung Walther König.

Schulz, M. (2022) "Givenchy launches phygital NFT collection as part of Bstroy collab", *Vogue Business*, 18 November. Available at: https://www.voguebusiness.com/technology/givenchy-launches-phygital-nft-collection-as-part-of-bstroy-collab (Accessed: 20 March 2023).

Serafin, A. (2022) "Past meets present: inside 30 Avenue Montaigne, Dior's new look Parisian flagship", *Wallpaper*, 19 August. Available at: https://www.wallpaper.com/fashion/dior-30-avenue-montaigne-paris-store-museum?utm_source=Selligent&utm_medium=email&utm_campaign=20220407_XWP-X_NWL_EO_Daily-Digest&utm_content=20220407_XWP-X_NWL_EO_Daily-Digest&utm_term=8793155&m_i=FCwv6UGZZcoKIL7ruSixKRMRGL51 5I8dYlE%2BiFGPNfQyDpt0c1mfkOEbt5gzlwFkSBAtWonbE7VQEBZ9BE HVRNhsGrZvNSaFFE&lrh=3d8c79b3364f9758b36d74eaccf9b416214d8f3 fb4e6a092d9684146bfdeb5c3&M_BT=38661145981656 (Accessed: 23 August 2022).

Shaw, S. (2021) "Virgil Abloh brings wearable art by Damien Hirst and Tetsuzo Okubo to Canary Yellow", *L'Officiel USA*, 5 February. Available at: https://www.lofficielusa.com/fashion/virgil-abloh-damien-hirst-tetsuzo-okubo-beverly-hirst-recycler-canary-yellow (Accessed: 27 March 2023).

Sinclair, I. (2023) "NFTs and luxury fashion: a conscious coupling", *L'Officiel USA*, 14 April. Available at: https://www.lofficielusa.com/fashion/nfts-luxury-fashion-collaborations-gucci-louis-vuitton (Accessed: 16 February 2023).

Smith, W.S. (2019) "What the rise of KAWS says about the art world's ailments", *Art in America*, 3 September. Available at: https://www.artnews.com/art-in-america/features/kaws-democratized-art-peddles-relatable-motifs-exhaustion-death-63649/ (Accessed: 12 March 2023).

Sotheby's (2018) *Portrait of a lady: Victoria Beckham's passion for old masters*. Available at: https://www.sothebys.com/en/videos/portrait-of-a-lady-victoria-beckhams-passion-for-old-masters (Accessed: 2 April 2023).

Sotheby's (2021) *Sotheby's Annual Wine & Spirits Auction Sales Hit Record $132 Million*, 21 December. Available at: https://www.sothebys.com/en/press/sothebys-annual-wine-spirits-auction-sales-hit-record-132-million (Accessed: 27 March 2023).

Sporn, S. (2019) "Victoria Beckham and the Frick toast to female old masters that changed art history", *Sotheby's*, 24 January. Available at: https://www.sothebys.com/en/slideshows/victoria-beckham-and-the-frick-toast-to-the-female-old-masters-that-changed-art-history?locale=en (Accessed: 20 April 2023).

Sporn, S. (2020) "Old Masters, new clothes: Highsnobiety drops Sotheby's streetwear line", *Sotheby's*, 13 January. Available at: https://www.sothebys.com/en/articles/highsnobiety-drops-old-master-paintings-streetwear-line (Accessed: 14 February 2023).

Stankovic, T., Tonner, A. and Wilson, A. (2016) "'I know what I like': parallel tastes in fine art consumption", *Advances in Consumer Research*, 44, pp. 343–347.

Suhrawardi, R. (2020) "Veuve Clicquot and Yayoi Kusama come together for a limited-edition bottle and sculpture", *Forbes*, 17 September. Available at: https://www.forbes.com/sites/rebeccasuhrawardi/2020/09/17/veuve-cliquot-and-yayoi-kusama-come-together-for-a-limited-edition-bottle-and-sculpture/ (Accessed: 13 February 2013).

The Editors of Artnews (2021) "The Macallan's latest masterpiece: auction and collaboration of the ages", *ARTnews*, 22 March. Available at: https://www.artnews.com/art-news/sponsored-content/the-macallan-artist-collaborations-12345861 (Accessed: 27 February 2022).

Tian, K. and Dong, L. (2010) *Consumer-Citizens of China: The Role of Foreign Brands in the Imagined Future China*. London: Routledge.

Trunzo, B., DeLeon, J. and Dreesen, E. (2018) *The New Luxury*. Available at: https://www.highsnobiety.com/p/the-new-luxury-whitepaper-highsnobiety/ (Accessed: 20 September 2023).

Ucollex (2021) "Jimmy Choo steps into digital collectibles", *Medium*, 12 October. Available at: https://medium.com/ucollex/jimmy-choo-steps-into-nfts-88af79d547fa (Accessed: 4 April).

Veblen, T. (2007) *The Theory of the Leisure Class*. Oxford: Oxford University Press.

Wang, X. (2014) "In pursuit of status: the rising consumerism of China's middle class", in A. Hulme (ed.) *The Changing Landscape of China's Consumerism*. Oxford: Chandos Publishing, pp.1–22.

Weiyun, T. (2021) "Hermès luxury brand exhibition goes off camera", *Shanghai Daily.com*, 27 March. Available at: https://archive.shine.cn/feature/Herms-luxury-brand-exhibition-goes-off-camera/shdaily.shtml (Accessed: 30 May 2022).

Wiesing, L. (2019) *A Philosophy of Luxury*. Translated by N.A. Roth. London: Routledge.

Williams, G.A. (2021) "Luxury's next frontier: live action role playing", *Jing Daily*, 18 May. Available at: https://jingdaily.com/live-action-role-playing-luxury-hermes-ferragamo/ (Accessed: 30 May 2022).

Wolf, J.R. Jr., Arkes, H.R. and Muhanna, W.A. (2006) "Do auction bidders 'really' want to win the item, or do they simply want to win?", 19 January. Available at: https://ssrn.com/abstract=764785.

Wu, W. (2020) "How mixing art and retail can work in China (and how it can't)", *Jing Daily Culture*, 24 July. Available at: https://jingculturecrypto.com/mixing-art-retail-can-work-in-china-jing-travel/ (Accessed: 23 February 2020).

Yotka, S. (2021) "Louis Vuitton's Stephen Sprouse collaboration turns 20 – and is still one of the best logo hacks around", *British Vogue*, 7 May. Available at: https://www.vogue.co.uk/fashion/article/louis-vuitton-stephen-sprouse-collaboration-20-years-later (Accessed: 15 March 2023).

5   Identities

The postmodern evolution of the market has exerted a substantial impact on the relationship between companies and consumers and, within it, on the way corporate players manage their identity.[1]

Whilst in a traditional marketplace companies and consumers mostly connect by virtue of spatial-temporal proximity, which allows consumers to develop an organic and direct knowledge of companies and their products, modern industrialisation and the more recent globalisation process have severed much of this relational immediacy: by delocalising their production and extending their network of outlets and service support worldwide, businesses have increasingly come to rely on third-party outsourcing (Balmer, 2010). In such a mediated market configuration branding becomes paramount for a company to retain and handle its connections with the market, orienting customers' corporate associations and product preferences, thus eventually ensuring the business existence and growth (Brown and Dacin, 1997; Balmer, 2010).

At the other end of the relationship, globalisation has impacted on the consumers' approach to products: confronted with the dilution of strong social ties and the great narratives of modern togetherness through political, religious or familial affiliation, postmodern consumers increasingly turn to the market as a space of identity construction, where through the access to goods, images and contents they define themselves and the reality they live in (Firat and Venkatesh, 1995; Bauman, 2004). As a result, in their purchase choices they will tend to appreciate the symbolic aspects of a product, at times over and above its functional attributes or performance (Santagata, 2004; Firat, 2023).

The market's penchant for such "semiotic goods" (Barrère and Santagata, 1999, p. 31) has prompted companies to pivot towards the release of outputs with unique features or imbued with compelling stories (Boltanski and Esquerre, 2020) and to articulate their brand promise as a rich symbolic ecosystem titillating consumers' senses and emotions: "brands that create worlds that strike consumers' imaginations, that inspire and provoke and stimulate, that help them interpret the world that surrounds them, will earn kudos and profits" (Holt, 2002, p. 87). In sourcing branding cues with a semantic charge, businesses often draw from their own history, values and expertise: branding

DOI: 10.4324/9781003274094-6

has hence moved from being product-related to include a company's culture and those corporate abilities (CA) underlying the creation of their products (Brown and Dacin, 1997).

In addition to the interaction with the consumers, over the past decades companies have reappraised their role against a more articulated "network of relations" (Balmer, Fukukawa and Gray, 2007, p. 12). The liberal tradition had conceived corporations' raison d'être as business for business, whereby companies would cater to customers with the ultimate aim of maximising their shareholders' returns – the only limits set by the relevant jurisdictional framework (Friedman, 1970). Starting from the 1950s, however, a different view has been consolidating, one posing that "business and society are interwoven rather than distinct entities" (Wood, 1991, p. 695). In consequence, organisations have widened their remit beyond economic profitability and legal compliance, assuming corporate social responsibility (CSR) towards multiple constituencies – inclusive of non-consuming stakeholders, non-human stakeholders such as the environment and future generations of stakeholders (Garvare and Johansson, 2010). Through the promotion of ethical practices and philanthropic contributions, companies seek to add another layer to their identity, fulfilling the social expectations of "a good corporate citizen" (Carroll, 1991, p. 42).[2]

In this context, for the past 40 years companies' engagement with the arts has played an instrumental role in defining both the CA and CSR prongs of their identity: businesses of different sizes and economic sectors have implemented art interventions, introducing individuals, processes and outputs from the art world to generate "spaces of possibility" (Berthoin Antal and Strauß, 2013, p. 32) within their organisation, stimulate employees' inventiveness and original thinking and initiate collaborative work practices. Art collecting is another initiative carried out by companies, and more than for its financial merits, for the corporate advantages in terms of workplace enhancement, workforce motivation and community involvement (Iley, 1984; Kottasz et al., 2008).

With specific reference to luxury brand and art collaborations, scholars have mainly detailed their impact on a product-branding level, as a strategic tool for luxury companies to elevate their products against the fashionisation of the industry while intensifying the aesthetic and emotional undertone of their branding communications (Jelinek, 2018; Koronaki, Kyrousi and Panigyrakis, 2018; Parguel, Delécolle and Mimouni Chaabane, 2020); advances have also been made in the analysis of the corporate underpinnings of collaborations (Baumgarth, 2018; Massi and Turrini, 2020).

Within this latter stream of research, the chapter invites us to re-examine these collaborative outputs and other art-related initiatives undertaken by luxury companies from the vantage point of the corporate context behind their creation. Emerging from the complex interaction between executives, creative directors, artists and art institutions, luxury brand and art collaborations not only testify to the radical shifts occurring in the creative leadership and management of luxury companies, but they are also redefining luxury businesses and the value they deliver in the postmodern market and within society at large.

Hyphenated creativity

Among semiotic goods, creative-based products are possibly the most valuable and valued as a result of the original inputs informing their aesthetic and functional features (Han, Forbes and Schaefer, 2021). This makes creativity, i.e., the ability to process external stimuli and ideas to generate something new, "a fundamental resource in post-modern society" (Santagata, 2004, p. 77) and a major factor of business differentiation and competitive advantage.

It is hardly surprising, therefore, that luxury companies enunciate creativity as one of their core CA: at least from 2002 luxury conglomerate LVMH includes in its annual reports the identifying tagline "passionate about creativity" (Donzé and Wubs, 2018; LVMH, 2021); during the Hermès shareholders' meeting in 2022, CEO and family member Axel Dumas paid homage to the House's foundations in "the deployment of amazing amounts of creativity fed by constant curiosity" (Danziger, 2022). Long-established luxury brands celebrate the creative genius of their founders and chief designers through dedicated storytelling and retail strategies (Dion and Arnould, 2011) and set up corporate archives and museums to ensure their legacy is accurately preserved and passed onto future generations of creatives (Lawry and Helm, 2014).

Many creatives, for their part, turn to art to nourish their visionary talent and inspire their practice: among the recent generations, Jonathan Anderson, Marc Jacobs, Raf Simons and Kim Jones are renowned art collectors; many undertake side artistic projects, for instance Hedi Slimane's photoshoot of Rolls-Royce for *Dazed* magazine (Hellqvist, 2010), Anderson's curated exhibition *Disobedient Bodies* at the Hepworth Wakefield (Batliwalla, 2017) and Jones' collaboration with Peter Harrington Rare Books and the estate of Jack Kerouac for a literary show on the Beat Generation (Diderich, 2021b).

Besides feeding back into their main work, these extra-curricular endeavours position designers' professional identity beyond their job description. Raf Simons, co-creative director of Prada, shies away from the label "fashion designer": "I never dreamed about it when I was a teenager. [...] there was interest in a lot of creative fields. Art, fashion, design, architecture" (Simons, in Morency and Obrist, 2020).

Late Virgil Abloh took this stance further. Akin to Simons, Abloh trained outside fashion, and during the years at the helm of Off-White and Louis Vuitton, he applied his fertile imagination in countless capsule collections with luxury and fast-moving consumer goods (FMCG) brands, cafés, museums, ballet companies, sport leagues, visual artists, musicians (Salessy and Marain, 2021). Abloh's protean activity as a DJ, artist and designer not only deeply resonated with Gen-Z consumers and their "unwillingness to be defined into one category" (Hoang, 2021), but it also fully sanctioned the figure of the hyphenated creative on a corporate level – so much so that Louis Vuitton appointed polymath Pharrell Williams as his successor (Cotton, 2023). Creative versatility has become a desirable asset for independent companies as well: Ramdane Touhami and Victoire de Taillac co-founded the niche beauty brand Buly and harnessed their diverse occupational backgrounds (DJ, interior designer and artist the former; ex-communications director of the concept store Colette the latter) to concoct a series of inspired artistic projects – from literary publications to a society for emerging artists (Fetto, 2018).

This finds echoes in the art world as well. In his incursions into fashion multi-media artist, Sterling Ruby has advocated against the "segregation of practice" (Ruby, in Dakhli, 2020) promoted by formal art education and disciplinary conventions (Caves, 2000): "for me, it doesn't matter whether I make a sculpture out of that fabric, or a pair of pants, or a big flag, or a theatre backdrop, or a jacket" (Ruby, in Fury, 2019). As a matter of fact, today's artists enjoy a greater expressive freedom, seamlessly articulating their unique vision across genres, disciplines and formats in both the artistic and commercial domains (Proctor, 2009).

As creative processes, luxury brand and art collaborations frequently display anti-utilitarian and fuzzy traits that defy the organisational tenets of resource efficiency and operational rationality (Barrère and Santagata, 1999; Weber, 2005). A few of them have sprung from the personal chemistry and aesthetic consonances between the brand creative and the artist: Kim Jones – already sharing with figurative artist Peter Doig alma mater Central Saint Martins and an active presence on the London creative scene – had the idea to involve Doig for Dior's Fall/Winter 2021 menswear collection "from talking to Peter Doig, from looking at his work" (Jones, in Fury, 2021); in the case of futuristic artist Hajime Sorayama, Jones paid a surprise visit to his studio to propose a collaboration the same day he attended the exhibition *Sorayama Explosion* at Nanzuka gallery in Tokyo (Artnet News, 2019); Raf Simons bonded with Sterling Ruby over his ceramics first, and later on over their common Dutch origins (Morency and Obrist, 2020); Stéphanie Busuttil-Janssen of Fondation César accepted working with Celine on a limited edition of pendants because of the distinctive aesthetics of creative director Heidi Slimane, whose 1960s–1970s Parisian flair reminded her of César Baldaccini's creative milieu (Brara, 2020).

In their unfolding these collaborations retained a certain spontaneous intimacy: Doig became an integral member of Dior's development team (Buck, 2021), as Busuttil-Janssen did with Slimane and his studio without any further contact with Celine (Brara, 2020); for Sorayama, working with Jones was simply about "two weirdos having fun" (Artnet News, 2019). When it came to commissioning Sterling Ruby and Roger Hiorns with the design of his Japanese stores, Raf Simons averted the stifling client-executor dynamic by giving them carte blanche: "Are you up for a project like that? Here are the keys" (Simons, in Morency and Obrist, 2020).

In some other cases collaborative projects stretch beyond the elective affinities between individuals and come to involve organisations at large. Multifaceted creative Hiroshi Fujiwara launched collaborations with Maserati and Loro Piana, among others. Whilst for Maserati the partnership with Fujiwara was perceived as a natural fit stemming from the shared "devot[ion] to innovation and creativity" (Maserati, no date), Loro Piana, at its very first experience with a collaboration, had instead to "open [...] up to Fujiwara's aesthetic" (d'Angelantonio, in Brara, 2021b).

From this perspective, executives have a leading role in a brand's "semiotic management" (Jeanneret in Mouratidou, 2020, p. 133), securing the alignment between creative activities and a company's identity: Aesop's creative director Marsha Meredith states that the programmatic mission set by CEO Michael O'Keeffe – "maintain and enhance our difference as we scale" – provides her with a clear blueprint to shape a collaborative agenda that is authentic and salient to the brand's DNA (Meredith, in Fetto, 2018).

Remo Ruffini, CEO and chairman of Moncler, has made strategic use of collaborations to reform the company's core identity of mountain apparel maker: "it was always in my mind to build a unique company [...] I knew we could do something different, innovative" (Ruffini, in BoF Team, 2019). In 2018 he launched the Moncler Genius Project, a recurrent series of capsule collections based on high-profile collaborations with design and artistic talents of the likes of Pierpaolo Piccioli, Jonathan Anderson, Alicia Keys, Hiroshi Fujiwara, Pharrell Williams (Rushford, 2023). The project had far-reaching implications: in order to encourage an environment where temporary creative teams could freely generate, bounce and test ideas, extensive changes were introduced in every corporate area, from the creation of cross-functional spaces to the adoption of an empowering management style (BoF Team, 2019).

More generally, the case of Moncler epitomises the renewed quest and interest of the luxury industry for creativity, with fashion houses like Helmut Lang, McQ and Jean Paul Gaultier adopting permeable business models based on guest creators or rotating creative directors (Milnes, 2017; Chitrakorn, 2021), or enlisting consultancies specialised in collaborations' scouting and management, such as ICNCLST and Just an Idea by Colette's former co-founder Sarah Andelman (Caruso, 2021; Tauer, 2022).

Collaborative outputs as culture creation

The dynamic interaction between multi-hyphenated creatives, visionary executives and artists often translates into imaginative outputs, articulated as multi-layered suites of activation or pioneering a new format altogether.

Deciding to preserve Colette's "spirit of curiosity" (Vaccarello, in Serafin, 2022) after its closure in 2017, Saint Laurent's creative director Anthony

Vaccarello established Saint Laurent Rive Droite: at Rive Droite, Vaccarello independently curates the selection of items on sale – rarities, comic books, vinyl records, collaborative editions with artists and designers – and liaises with galleries and cultural institutions to organise in-store artistic events (Serafin, 2022).

During his tenure as creative director at Gucci, Alessandro Michele replaced the brand's Spring/Summer 2021 fashion show with #GucciFest, a digital film festival where 15 independent designers presented a short film of their collection; Gucci contributed with *Ouverture of Something That Never Ended*, a 7-episode series with conceptual references to art and music, written and co-directed by Gus Van Sant and starring artist Silvia Calderoni and musicians Florence Welch, Harry Styles and Billie Eilish (Hess, 2020).

Media brand Highsnobiety has been trialling content festivals: held during the Miami Art Week and Paris Fashion Week respectively, HIGHArt and Not in Paris present a multi-media programme where exclusive brand and artist collaborations are featured in pop-up store/museum shows (co-curated with Sarah Andelman and Jeanne-Salomé Rochat, head of brand and creative at Art Basel), magazines and live events (Barker, 2021; Ferere, 2021).

The resonance and relevance of these activities transcend the actual output released. The cornucopia of collaborative products signed by Virgil Abloh – from the T-shirts and hoodies celebrating the Louvre's exhibition on Leonardo da Vinci in 2019 to the reusable Soma bottle for Evian – can be in fact considered meta-merchandise pointing to the act of playful reinterpretation beyond the objects' class or materiality: "with someone like Virgil, it's not about what the product is anymore. [...] It's in a field of its own — definition doesn't matter" (Li, in Milnes, 2018). Film show #GucciFest and Highsnobiety's content festivals dramatise the human experience of fashion on the premise that "fashion exists as much as content as it exists as clothing" (Bettridge, in Diderich, 2021a). In the same vein, the final output of Moncler Genius is for Ruffini "not only a product, [...] not only a collection, it's an idea" (Ruffini, in BoF Team, 2019): in this example, the Moncler Genius production has branched into a Spotify podcast and a series of public events such as the panel discussion held in 2019 during the Hong Kong Arts Month, where Hiroshi Fujiwara, art critic Hans Ulrich Obrist and Hypebeast founder Kevin Ma explored the role of creativity in digital society (Hypebeast, 2019).

By treating their outputs as "a means, not the end" (Morency, 2021), luxury companies act de facto as content creators, enhancing through the release of products the semantic richness of their brand universe (Chitrakorn, 2021; Morency, 2022). Saint Laurent Rive Droite is Vaccarello's "fun" and "personal" place of expression (Vaccarello, in Bizet, 2019); nonetheless, the curated collections of objects and events are ultimately conveying the essence of Saint Laurent: "it also shows how Saint Laurent is more than just a luxury brand; it's an attitude" (Vaccarello, in Bizet, 2019).

Furthermore, the continuous, prolific and multifaceted cross-pollination with the art world ends up placing luxury corporations in a much wider domain than simply content creation, namely that of culture production. If creativity arises from the two-way interaction between human beings and the specific socio-historical circumstances they come to operate in (Rudowicz, 2003), as one of its most distinctive expressions art has the intrinsic power to manifest the zeitgeist of its time, "giving life and colo[u]r to the significant" (Cooley, in Foster, 1989, p. 2), challenging the status quo or envisioning an alternative reality altogether. In creating a basis for their departments and external collaborators to explore different creative avenues, luxury brands ultimately come to stand at the epicentre of culture generation, where they facilitate themes and practices of reflection about a society's founding ideals, values and beliefs, foster present and future generations of creatives and thinkers, ultimately promoting and preserving their outputs. From this perspective, the activity of luxury brands is bound to unfold "more like what museums do than what vloggers do" (Bettridge, 2021), getting them closer to becoming fully fledged cultural institutions.

This rewrites the corporate identity agenda of executives and creative directors. In assuming the creative leadership of Loewe in 2013, Jonathan Anderson shifted the brand's positioning away from the expected but tired concept of "luxury". Instead, he leveraged his personal interest in crafts and the artisanal origins of the company to reimagine Loewe as a collaborative workshop where craftsmen and artists dialogue with the brand through different material languages (Browne, 2017). Through the celebration of artisanal creativity, Anderson has drawn a powerfully imaginative *fil rouge* connecting the brand's products and the artistic programmes of the Loewe Foundation and Loewe Craft Prize. This, in turn, has initiated a profound, collective conversation about the art and the act of making, eventually activating Loewe as a "cultural" brand (Anderson, in Yotka, 2020).

The cultural drift characterising many luxury brands' corporate identity more widely marks a further evolution in the postmodern relationship between companies and consumers. With the advent of social media and digital marketplaces re-establishing a direct link between companies and consumers based on networked connectivity rather than physical contiguity (Castells, 2001; Burrows and Beer, 2013), consumers have progressively come to rely on luxury brands not only as producers of semantic goods but also as tastemakers and advisors on what is meaningful and relevant today.

Between outputs and outreach: The identity tension of luxury brands

In developing their product-based art collaborations, luxury brands have on occasion released outputs with a public purpose: through its namesake foundation, Jimmy Choo donated the sale proceeds of the one-of-a-kind non-fungible token (NFT) designed with Haze (Chapter 4) to Women for Women International, non-profit aiding female war survivors; the set of 15 NFTs created by Givenchy and multidisciplinary artist Chito supported The Ocean Cleanup in its mission to fight marine plastic pollution (Cantarini, 2021).

At a corporate level, luxury companies have carved a pathway specific to art-related causes, sponsoring underfunded sectors such as the performing arts – as exemplified by Dolce & Gabbana and Giorgio Armani's patronage of La Scala opera house in Milan (Muret, 2015; Salibian, 2021) or Chanel financing the Opening Gala of the dance season at the Opéra national de Paris (Chanel, 2023) – or vulnerable categories of artists – from the Max Mara Art Prize for Women offering British female artists a six-month residency in Italy and dedicated exhibitions at the Whitechapel Gallery and Collezione Maramotti (Whitechapel Gallery, 2023) to the Rolex Mentor and Protégé Arts Initiative, pairing emerging artists with a master in their discipline for a one-year tutelage (Rolex, 2023).

The art patronage of luxury companies can take tangible shape in the establishment of art foundations and museums or the restoration of historical landmarks. This sheds light on companies' role as active members of their communities: Fondazione Prada, a repurpose project of a distillery compound in a once-deprived area of Milan, represented a breakthrough from the traditional cloistered palazzo museum of the city centre, which had traditionally kept the access to art exclusive to the urban élites (Abrahams, 2015); the Fondation Louis Vuitton, built on a parkland plot of the Bois de Boulogne, was conceived by architect Frank Gehry as "a magnificent vessel in Paris that symbolises France's cultural vocation" (Gehry, in LVMH, 2023) and that could also "be part of the incredible legacy of the park" (Gehry, in Davidson, 2015). A tribute to the Fendi family's city of origin, Alda Fendi restored Palace Rhinoceros in Rome, close to the Tiber bank where the Eternal City was founded, and turned it into a cultural and artistic hub (Reginato, 2019); the suggestive link between water, Rome, and Fendi was also the leading theme of Fendi's corporate project Fendi for Fountains, which, starting from the iconic Trevi Fountain in 2015, would restore four other fountains over the following four years (Zargani, 2019).

It is generally acknowledged that pursuing philanthropic causes is conducive to corporate strategic differentiation and financial optimisation (Carroll and Shabana, 2010). For luxury brands, the patronage of art and culture represents a powerful means to establish a strong reputational presence among a wider audience than simply the paying customer, as explained by Dominique Perrin, founder of the Fondation Cartier: "the Fondation has given Cartier a positive image in the eyes of people who are not interested in jewellery or who would never in a thousand years wear a Cartier bijou. But now they look at Cartier more positively, with respect" (Perrin, in Proctor, 2009). There are marketing and cost benefits too: Prada makes regular use of Fondazione Prada and the restored Palace Rong Zhai in Shanghai for their fashion shows

(Qiu, 2019); La Scala and the Trevi Fountain hosted benefactors Dolce & Gabbana and Fendi's shows in 2015 and 2016, respectively.

The more luxury companies present themselves as influential art stewards and mentors, however, the more they are bound to experience an identity tension between their for-profit roots and their emerging role as cultural entrepreneurs (Knox and Casulli, 2023), which set its focus on "the art itself and the creative process" (Klamer, 2011, p. 154) over any economic outcome.

This tension is reflected in the management of art-related projects, with luxury companies oscillating between the separation of the artistic from the commercial and their integration into the corporate structure. A number of luxury brands' art foundations have originated from the personal interests of their owners and/or founders – Bernard Arnault, François Pinault, Miuccia Prada etc. – or have been built up on their private art collections, like Collezione Maramotti (Pechman, 2015). They nonetheless operate as self-standing entities: for Hervé Chandès, general director of Fondation Cartier, being autonomous from the brand protects the Fondation's "artistic independence" (Chandès, in Chen, 2015); on similar grounds, Miuccia Prada has steered clear from seeking sponsors for Fondazione Prada (Chu, 2015). Other small-scale, brand-led art initiatives are instead incorporated under ad hoc departments and professional capacities: for its namesake art support programme, Audemars Piguet has appointed in-house curators (Brara, 2021a), while dance supporter Van Cleef & Arpels has a specific division of dance and culture programmes (Silver, 2022). Chanel created in 2020 the department of Arts and Culture: currently directed by former Serpentine Gallery director Yana Peel, the department oversees the Maison's artistic portfolio, from the Chanel Next Prize to the partnerships with London's National Portrait Gallery, Los Angeles' Underground Museum and Paris' Centre Pompidou (Riley-Smith, 2021).

The outward identification of luxury brands as community benefactors is often characterised by a certain scepticism about the genuineness of their commitment, which is likely to be perceived as tokenistic or instrumental to project a more noble corporate self (Balmer, 2008; Wong and Dhanesh, 2017). One line of criticism specifically addresses the public impact of corporate art foundations or sponsorships: the flamboyant architecture of the Fondation Louis Vuitton, the very first privately funded cultural institution in France (Chen, 2015), has been interpreted as "an explicit monument to the anti-democratic, neoliberal ethos of our increasingly unequal times when rich individuals and corporations feel entitled to trample us with architectural bling" (Buchanan, in Davidson, 2015), and that of Fondazione Prada "a play between the idea of private wealth and public display [...] in such a manner that has proved to be too much for the conservative disposition of some" (Abrahams, 2015); Tod's contribution to the restoration of the Colosseum has sparked debates on the Disneyfication of cultural heritage (Faiola, 2014). This reflects the commonly held view that art and culture, as emerging from and feeding into the moral, intellectual and aesthetic values of a society, pertain to the public domain, hence governments should act as their financial and institutional enablers – not private ventures (Klamer, 2011).

It is irrefutable that the prominence assumed by luxury corporations in the public sphere is a consequence of neoliberal deregulation, and more specifically of governments' general disinvestment into art and culture coupled with the progressive encouragement of private sponsorship (OECD, 2022), as in the case of the Italian Art Bonus, granting to private sector organisations a tax credit equal to 65 per cent of their contributions to cultural heritage (Art Bonus, 2023). By the same token, such incentives can also reconfigure the interplay between public and private institutions (Mazzucato, 2022) in the light of an approach to postmodernity where "post-" becomes an opportunity for new value creation instead of inherited fate.

CASE

"Dolce Vita 4.0": The Roman patronage of Bulgari

Rome is not only artistic and architectural inspiration but also our […] Dolce Vita 4.0

(Jean-Christophe Babin [CPP-Luxury, 2019])

In 2020 more than 90 marbles of the Torlonia collection were unveiled to the public after decades of neglect in an exhibition organised at Villa Caffarelli in Rome and curated by archaeologists Salvatore Settis and Carlo Gasparri in collaboration with David Chipperfield Architects Milano (Imam, 2020).

Among the most prestigious private collections of Graeco-Roman art rivalling the Vatican Museums, the corpus of Torlonia marbles consists of 620 sculptural pieces – busts, reliefs, vases, sarcophagi, vases – that the princes of Torlonia, administrators of the Vatican finances over the 18th and 19th centuries, gathered through acquisitions from other aristocratic families in lieu of debts and findings from archaeological excavations in their Roman properties (Itzkowitz, 2020).

The Torlonia collection had been "Rome's best kept secret" (Imam, 2020) since 1976, when Prince Alessandro Torlonia decided to close the namesake museum and store the marbles away in one of the family's villas. After an allegedly thorny negotiation with the Italian government, 40 years later the Fondazione Torlonia agreed to finally put the works on display (Imam, 2020).

The exhibition project, however, only came to full fruition thanks to Bulgari and its financial support towards the restoration of the marbles.

For the Roman haute-jewellery brand, the restoration of the Torlonia marbles was part of an ambitious corporate programme aimed at preserving the architectonic and artistic landmarks of the Eternal City: in 2014 Bulgari had sponsored the renovation of the Spanish Steps, followed one year later by the restoration of the polychrome mosaic of the Caracalla Baths and in 2019 by the pledge to reopen Area Sacra, an ancient Roman complex in Largo di Torre Argentina (LVMH, 2019a). In the same year of the Torlonia marbles' exhibition, Bulgari signed an agreement with the Roman municipality for the relighting of the Ara Pacis: in announcing the alliance, then-mayor Virginia Raggi saluted Bulgari's "renewed commitment for the enhancement of the cultural heritage of our city" (Raggi, in Bulgari, 2020).

As a matter of fact, these initiatives place Bulgari not merely as the sponsor footing the bills but also as an influential private player in the otherwise publicly managed cultural preservation of Rome, one of the most iconic cities in the world. Bulgari's restoration of the Torlonia marbles, to give an example, pushed the Italian institutions to find a permanent home to the collection after the exhibition's global tour. In 2021 the minister of culture Dario Franceschini and the president of Lazio region Nicola Zingaretti signed a "valorisation agreement" for Palazzo Silvestri-Rivaldi as a potential location for the collection: in a rare instance of cross-governmental cooperation, the Italian state pledged €40 millions to restore the palace, with Lazio region taking charge of its urbanistic regeneration and activation at a community level (Giraud, 2021).

Considerations

Greek and Roman culture runs deep in the vein of Bulgari, which was founded in Rome in 1884 by Greek jeweller Sotirios Voulgaris. It took, however, the vision of current CEO Jean-Christophe Babin to bring Bulgari's corporate identity into a compelling and encompassing articulation.

French-born Babin joined Bulgari from Tag Heuer in 2013, two years after the acquisition of the brand by French conglomerate LVMH: up until that moment, Bulgari had been family-owned and -managed, and with CEO and family member Francesco Trapani had initiated its expansion across different product categories and sectors (de la Merced and Alderman, 2011).

In taking over, Babin looked to develop a first-hand, deep understanding of Bulgari at the intersection between place and time: "Bulgari is very Roman brand. Two great cultures – Roman and Greek – organically consolidated to form it. [...] I had to feel the personality of the Eternal City, to ramble through its streets, take another look at the architecture and ancient monuments. Paolo and Nicola Bulgari – the third generation of the brand's founder – helped me a lot" (Babin, in Khnychkin, 2014). Babin's *thick* – almost anthropological – approach was certainly spurred by a longstanding bond with Italy going back to his teenage years, which in turn informed his ability to capture and appreciate the spirit of the place and its influences on the colours, shapes and workmanship of Bulgari, which in turn sublimated in the Italian artisanal principle of "*bello benfatto* (beautiful and well crafted)" (CPP-Luxury, 2019; Mansour, 2020).

Through Babin's numerous interviews and active presence on the media, this view has consolidated into a "Dolce Vita 4.0" narrative, providing the French CEO a loom to seamlessly interweave the brand's identity and CA with its CSR implementations. First, Babin treats jewellery as a proper art form, hence making Bulgari's support of arts and culture an expected act of the company "giving back to its community" (Blatter, 2018).

In this context, Rome is acknowledged as Bulgari's "generous muse" (Babin, in Bulgari, 2020): while Roman vestiges have inspired Bulgari's distinctive designs – from the B.Zero1 line recalling the dynamic shape of the Colosseum to the Monete collection integrating ancient coins, the Roman/ Italian workmanship has percolated to shape the corporate culture globally: "I believe everyone in the company is proud to be Roman, whether you're Japanese, American or South African – they are proud to participate as an ambassador of Italian excellence through Bulgari" (Babin, in BoF Team, 2020).

It is in a spirit of gratitude that Roman philanthropic projects become "gift[s]" (Babin, in LVMH, 2019a) bestowed to the Eternal City, though at the same time strategically designed to emphasise Bulgari's "cultural roots" (Babin, in LVMH, 2019b): the Spanish Steps' project was meant to celebrate Bulgari's 130th anniversary and one of the brand's early boutiques in the close-by Via dei Condotti; the restoration of the pavements of the Caracalla Baths alluded to the Diva's Dream line, which reproduced their fan-shaped decorative motifs; the Ara Pacis is adjacent to the Bulgari Roman hotel, which opened in 2022 (Mansour, 2020).

Another stream of Bulgari's Roman patronage celebrates the movie-making tradition of the city through partnerships with film festivals, from Tribeca in New York to Toronto and Shanghai (Blatter, 2018). In 2021 Bulgari produced with Tribeca Studios a series of short docufilms on the series *Female Trailblazers*: one of them is *Lot 448*, following art detective Lynda Albertson in her mission to prevent the auction sale of a looted Etruscan antefix (Bulgari, 2021). Albertson's attempts prove, alas, unsuccessful. In a twist of events, however, Bulgari intervenes to buy the antefix on behalf of Italy and bring the important relic back home. Already patron of the Italian heritage, the identity of Bulgari is here further glamourised by being portrayed as the righteous hero of the day.

Notes

1 Corporate identity is commonly defined as the set of traits representing a company's core structure, culture, skillset, practices and operations; corporate brand identity refers instead to how those traits are perceived and interpreted by the stakeholders:

"corporate brand identities exist in our minds; corporate identities inhabit organisations" (Balmer, 2010, p. 181). The internal actors of an organisation – the ownership, management, leaders and staff – constantly negotiate its corporate identity against political, economic and market forces (Balmer and Gray, 2003; Balmer, Fukukawa and Gray, 2007), and communicate it to external stakeholders through multiple touchpoints so to align what the organisation is, or would like to be, with what the stakeholders see or infer (Cheney and Christensen, 2001; Abratt and Kleyn, 2012). From this viewpoint, corporate identity and corporate brand identity are broader constructs than the product brand, which mostly concerns with the presentation and promotion of a company's outputs (Balmer and Gray, 2003).

2 Increased scrutiny from the public and tightening regulatory policies on corporate transparency and accountability have shed light on the deficiencies behind the implementation of CSR, with many stressing how the discretionary nature of companies' charitable programmes defeats the essence of the moral act, ontologically purposeless and spontaneous (Matten and Crane, 2005; Bauman, 2008). The very concept of corporate citizenship is being challenged to be just a cosmetic rebrand of this self-serving philanthropy rather than a comprehensive agenda pushing organisations towards less comfortable arenas of civic and civil action (Matten and Crane, 2005; Waddock, 2007; Aßländer and Curbach, 2014).

Bibliography

Abrahams, T. (2015) "Fondazione Prada in Milan by OMA", *The Architectural Review*, 21 September. Available at: https://www.architectural-review.com/today/fondazione-prada-in-milan-by-oma (Accessed: 4 June 2023).

Abratt, R. and Kleyn, N. (2012) "Corporate identity, corporate branding and corporate reputations: reconciliation and integration", *European Journal of Marketing*, 46/7–8, pp. 1048–1063. Available at: https://doi.org/10.1108/03090561211230197.

Art Bonus (2023) *Art Bonus: English Brief*. Available at: https://artbonus.gov.it/english-brief.html (Accessed: 2 October 2023).

Artnet News (2019) "Why Dior turned to hyperreal Japanese sculptor Hajime Sorayama for its futuristic new men's collection", *Artnet News*, 17 June. Available at: https://news.artnet.com/art-world/hajime-dorayama-kim-jones-dior-1562881 (Accessed: 24 July 2023).

Aßländer, M.S. and Curbach, J. (2014) "The corporation as citoyen? Towards a new understanding of corporate citizenship", *Journal of Business Ethics*, 120/4, pp. 541–554. Available at: http://dx.doi.org/10.1007/s10551-013-2004-8.

Balmer, J.M.T. (2008) "Identity based views of the corporation", *European Journal of Marketing*, 42/9–10, pp. 879–906. Available at: https://doi.org/10.1108/03090560810891055.

Balmer, J.M.T. (2010) "Explicating corporate brands and their management: reflections and directions from 1995", *Journal of Brand Management*, 18/3, pp. 180–196. Available at: https://doi:10.1057/bm.2010.46.

Balmer, J.M.T., Fukukawa, K. and Gray, E.R. (2007) "The nature and management of ethical corporate identity: a commentary on corporate identity, corporate social responsibility and ethics", *Journal of Business Ethics*, 76/1, pp. 7–15. Available at: https://doi.org/10.1007/s10551-006-9278-z.

Balmer, J.M.T. and Gray, E.R.(2003) "Corporate brands: what are they? What of them?", *European Journal of Marketing*, 37/7–8, pp. 972–997. Available at: https://doi.org/10.1108/03090560310477627.

Barker, T. (2021) "Our HIGHArt Museum store without the museum is officially open in Miami", *Highsnobiety*, 1 December. Available at: https://www.highsnobiety.com/p/highart-miami-pop-up/ (Accessed: 30 May 2022).

Barrère, C. and Santagata, W. (1999) "Defining art: from the Brancusi Trial to the economics of artistic semiotic goods", *International Journal of Arts Management*, 1/2, pp. 28–38.

Batliwalla, N. (2017) "Disobedient bodies: Jonathan Anderson in conversation", *Sotheby's*, 10 March. Available at: https://www.sothebys.com/en/articles/disobedient-bodies-jonathan-anderson-in-conversation (Accessed: 7 June 2023).

Bauman, Z. (2004) *Work, Consumerism and the New Poor*. Maidenhead: McGraw-Hill Education.

Bauman, Z. (2008) *Does Ethics Have a Chance in a World of Consumers?* Cambridge: Harvard University Press.

Baumgarth, C. (2018) "Brand management and the world of the arts: collaboration, co-operation, co-creation, and inspiration", *The Journal of Product and Brand Management*, 27/3, pp. 237–248. Available at: https://doi.org/10.1108/JPBM-03-2018-1772.

Berthoin Antal, A. and Strauß, A. (2013) *Artistic Interventions in Organisations: Finding Evidence of Values-added [Creative Clash Report]*. Berlin: WZB. Available at: https://www.wzb.eu/system/files/docs/dst/wipo/effects_of_artistic_interventions_final_report.pdf.

Bettridge, T. (2021) *How Content Ate Marketing*, 28 January [Highsnobiety Newsletter].

Bizet, C. (2019) "Most brands are too scared to shock", *System Magazine*. Available at: https://system-magazine.com/issues/issue-13/saint-laurent-rive-droite (Accessed: 7 September 2023).

Blatter, L.C. (2018) "Bulgari's chief focuses on art, culture and experiences", *Penta*, 30 April. Available at: https://www.barrons.com/articles/bulgaris-chief-focuses-on-art-culture-and-experiences-1525120380 (Accessed: 10 July 2013).

BoF Team (2019) "At Moncler, embedding reinvention", *Business of Fashion*, 11 December. Available at: https://www.businessoffashion.com/articles/luxury/moncler-company-culture-embedding-reinvention/ (Accessed: 9 July 2023).

BoF Team (2020) "At Bulgari, infusing global innovation with local heritage", *Business of Fashion*, 16 March. Available at: https://www.businessoffashion.com/articles/workplace-talent/bulgari-ceo-interview-jean-christophe-babin-global-innovation-local-heritage/ (Accessed: 8 September 2023).

Boltanski, L. and Esquerre, A. (2020) *Enrichment: A Critique of Commodities*. Translated by C. Porter. Cambridge: Polity Press.

Brara, N. (2020) "How the work of the late French Nouveau Réalisme pioneer César lives on through a new series of pendants", *Artnet News*, 9 July. Available at: https://news.artnet.com/style/cesar-celine-collaboration-1893171 (Accessed: 15 May 2023).

Brara, N. (2021a) "'We're always looking for different perspectives': Audemars Piguet's in-house curators on the watchmaker's art commissions", *Artnet News*, 12 February. Available at: https://news.artnet.com/art-world/audemars-piguet-curators-interview-1942708 (Accessed: 15 October 2022).

Brara, N. (2021b) "Loro Piana teams up with Japanese visual artist and streetwear designer Hiroshi Fujiwara for their first-ever creative collaboration", *Artnet News*, 19 October. Available at: https://news.artnet.com/style/loro-piana-2021955 (Accessed: 24 July 2023).

Brown, T.J. and Dacin, P.A. (1997) "The company and the product: corporate associations and consumer product responses", *Journal of Marketing*, 61/1, pp. 68–84. Available at: https://doi.org/10.2307/1252190.

Browne, A. (2017) "He's crafty", *W*, 46/4, p. 106.

Buck, L. (2021) "From canvas to catwalk: Dior turns Peter Doig's atmospheric paintings into menswear collection", *The Art Newspaper*, 25 January. Available at: https://nam10.safelinks.protection.outlook.com/?url=https%3A%2F%2Fwww.theartnewspaper.com%2Fblog%2Fpeter-doig-dog-sweater-dior&data=04%7C01%7Cf. carlotto%40sothebysinstitute.com%7C98c3a17d57154b5f396908d8c1f04fb5% 7Cb0067f83bfe14e9e8a2c51eed71010d2%7C0%7C0%7C637472585153204959% 7CUnknown%7CTWFpbGZsb3d8eyJWIjoiMC4wLjAwMDAiLCJQIjoiV2luMzIiL CJBTil6lk1haWwiLCJXVCI6Mn0%3D%7C1000&sdata=3mCMLBxl7ED7n v7vSGRMJ1W%2BD%2FEsxQhRku5G9%2FG5BVQ%3D&reserved=0 (Accessed: 8 June 2023).

Bulgari (2020) *The Ara Pacis Will Be Seen in a New Light, Thanks to the Contribution from Bulgari*, 2 July [Press release]. Available at: https://mediakit.bulgari.com/ bulgarihotels/wp-content/uploads/2020/07/cs-relamping-Ara-Pacis-MOD-JCB_ EN-1-luglio.pdf (Accessed: 20 September 2023).

Bulgari (2021) *Tribeca Film Festival 2021*. Available at: https://www.bulgari.com/en-gb/stories/tribeca-film-festival-2021.html (Accessed: 20 September 2023).

Burrows, R. and Beer, D. (2013) "Rethinking space: urban informatics and the sociological imagination", in K. Orton-Johnson and N. Prior (eds.) *Digital Sociology: Critical Perspectives*. Basingstoke: Palgrave Macmillan, pp. 61–78.

Cantarini, G. (2021) "Givenchy is auctioning NFTs with artist Chito", *L'Officiel USA*, 19 November. Available at: https://www.lofficielusa.com/fashion/givenchy-chito-nft-charity-auction-ocean-cleanup (Accessed: 19 August 2023).

Carroll, A.B. (1991) "The pyramid of corporate social responsibility: toward the moral management of organizational stakeholders", *Business Horizons*, 34/4, pp. 39–48. Available at: https://doi.org/10.1016/0007-6813(91)90005-G.

Carroll, A.B. and Shabana, K.M. (2010) "The business case for corporate social responsibility: a review of concepts, research and practice", *International Journal of Management Reviews*, 12/1, pp. 85–105. Available at: https://doi.org/10.1111/j.1468-2370.2009.00275.x.

Caruso, C. (2021) "The woman behind collaborations: an interview with Sarah Andelman", *NSS Magazine*, 20 April. Available at: https://www.nssmag.com/en/fashion/26005/sarah-andelman-colette-just-an-idea (Accessed: 7 June 2023).

Castells, M. (2001) *The Internet Galaxy: Reflections on the Internet, Business, and Society*. New York: Oxford University Press.

Caves, R.E. (2000) *Creative Industries: Contracts between Art and Commerce*. Cambridge: Harvard University Press.

Chanel (2023) *Grand Patron of the Paris Opera, Chanel Supports the Opening Gala*, 23 September [YouTube]. Available at: https://www.youtube.com/watch?v=Ju_AoU4AEZE (Accessed: 30 September 2023).

Chen, V. (2015) "Luxury brands are setting up their own museums to preserve heritage and honour arts", *Style*, 6 August. Available at: https://www.scmp.com/magazines/style/article/1845191/luxury-brands-are-setting-their-own-museums-preserve-heritage-and (Accessed: 19 August 2022).

Cheney, G. and Christensen, L.T. (2001) "Organizational identity: linkages between internal and external communication", in F.M. Jablin and L.L. Putnam (eds.) *The New Handbook of Organizational Communication: Advances in Theory, Research, and Methods*. London: Sage Publications, pp. 231–269.

Chitrakorn, K. (2021) "Luxury is culture now. Here's how", *Vogue Business*, 16 July. Available at: https://www.voguebusiness.com/companies/how-luxury-brands-become-cultural-curators-gucci-saint-laurent-vetements (Accessed: 12 July 2023).

Chu, C. (2015) "Take a look inside Miuccia Prada and Patrizio Bertelli's new Fondazione Prada", *Artnet News*, 6 April. Available at: https://news.artnet.com/art-world/take-a-look-inside-fondazione-prada-285271 (Accessed: 3 September 2023).

Cotton, C. (2023) "How art and fashion collaborations have evolved over the decades", *Art in America*, 15 November. Available at: https://www.artnews.com/art-in-america/features/evolving-landscape-art-fashion-collaborations-1234686637/ (Accessed: 24 November 2023).

CPP-Luxury (2019) "Bulgari is an irresistible narrative and not isolated products, Jean-Christophe Babin", *CPPLuxury*, 18 March. Available at: https://cpp-luxury.com/bvlgari-is-an-irresistible-narrative-and-not-isolated-products-jean-christophe-babin-exclusive-interview/ (Accessed: 10 July 2023).

Dakhli, M. (2020) "The telling rooms of Sterling Ruby", *Highsnobiety*. Available at: https://www.highsnobiety.com/p/the-telling-rooms-of-sterling-ruby/ (Accessed: 5 June 2023).

Danziger, P.N. (2022) "Hermès looks beyond bags to stores, home and the metaverse for growth", *Forbes*, 25 April. Available at: https://www.forbes.com/sites/pamdanziger/2022/04/25/herms-looks-beyond-bags-to-stores-home-and-the-metaverse-for-growth/?sh=716c0b995643 (Accessed: 16 July 2023).

Davidson, J. (2015) "Why Frank Gehry's Fondation Louis Vuitton building is a masterpiece", *Vulture*, 25 March. Available at: https://www.vulture.com/2015/03/why-gehrys-new-paris-building-is-a-masterpiece.html (Accessed: 25 September 2023).

de la Merced, M.J. and Alderman, L. (2011) "For Bulgari, LVMH deal pays way to growth", *The New York Times*, 7 March. Available at: https://archive.nytimes.com/dealbook.nytimes.com/2011/03/07/for-bulgari-lvmh-deal-paves-way-to-growth/ (Accessed: 10 September 2023).

Diderich, J. (2021a) "Media people: Thom Bettridge of Highsnobiety", *WWD*, 19 January. Available at: https://wwd.com/feature/thom-bettridge-highsnobiety-not-in-paris-ii-platform-1234700212/ (Accessed: 8 June 2023).

Diderich, J. (2021b) "Dior Men's collection will pay tribute to 'On The Road' author Jack Kerouac", *WWD*, 9 December. Available at: https://wwd.com/fashion-news/fashion-features/dior-men-pre-fall-show-london-tribute-jack-kerouac-on-the-road-beat-generation-1235013034/ (Accessed: 10 May 2023).

Dion, D. and Arnould, E. (2011) "Retail luxury strategy: assembling charisma through art and magic", *Journal of Retailing*, 87/4, pp. 502–520. Available at: https://doi.org/10.1016/j.jretai.2011.09.001.

Donzé, P.Y. and Wubs, B. (2018) "LVMH: storytelling and organizing creativity in luxury and fashion", in R.L. Blaszczyk and V. Pouillard (eds.) *European Fashion: The Creation of a Global Industry*. Manchester: Manchester University Press, pp. 63–85.

Faiola, A. (2014) "The fall of Rome? Italy's fears that corporate-sponsored restoration projects will lead to the Disneyfication of its cultural heritage", *The Independent*,

8 September. Available at: https://www.independent.co.uk/news/world/europe/the-fall-of-rome-italy-s-fears-that-corporatesponsored-restoration-projects-will-lead-to-the-disneyfication-of-its-cultural-heritage-9717010.html (Accessed: 27 September 2023).

Ferere, C. (2021) "The digital exhibition 'Not in Paris' is going to Paris for the first time", *Forbes*, 15 June. Available at: https://www.forbes.com/sites/cassellferere/2021/06/15/the-digital-exhibition-not-in-paris-is-going-to-paris-for-the-first-time/ (Accessed: 27 July 2023).

Fetto, F. (2018) "From Aesop to DS & Durga, the brands that mix beauty with culture", *Vogue*, 20 October. Available at: https://www.vogue.co.uk/article/the-culture-of-beauty-arts (Accessed: 29 May 2023).

Firat, A.F. (2023) "Contemporary implications of aestheticization", in A. Joy (ed.) *New Directions in Art, Fashion, and Wine: Sustainability, Digitalization, and Artification.* Lanham: Lexington Books, pp. 29–42.

Firat, A.F. and Venkatesh, A. (1995) "Liberatory postmodernism and the reenchantment of consumption", *Journal of Consumer Research*, 22/3, pp. 239–267. Available at: https://doi.org/10.1086/209448.

Foster, A.W. (1989) "Introduction", in A.W. Foster and J.R. Blau (eds.) *Art and Society: Readings in the Sociology of the Arts.* Albany: State University of New York Press.

Friedman, M. (1970) "The social responsibility of business is to increase its profits", *New York Times Magazine*, 13 September. Available at: https://www.nytimes.com/1970/09/13/archives/a-friedman-doctrine-the-social-responsibility-of-business-is-to.html (Accessed: 17 July 2023).

Fury, A. (2019) "Sterling Ruby, the lauded American artist turns fashion designer", *Financial Times*, 13 June. Available at: https://www.ft.com/content/f9de291a-85f0-11e9-b861-54ee436f9768 (Accessed: 18 November 2020).

Fury, A. (2021) "'Dior Doig': Kim Jones speaks on his collaboration with Peter Doig", *AnOther Magazine*, 23 January. Available at: https://www.anothermag.com/another-man/13068/dior-doig-kim-jones-speaks-on-his-collaboration-with-peter-doig-aw21-fw21-mens (Accessed: 12 June 2023).

Garvare, R. and Johansson, P. (2010) "Management for sustainability: a stakeholder theory", *Total Quality Management & Business Excellence*, 21/7, pp. 737–744. Available at: https://doi.org/10.1080/14783363.2010.483095.

Giraud, C. (2021) "Finalmente si restaura Palazzo Silvestri-Rivaldi a Roma. Arriva la Collezione Torlonia?", *Artribune*, 16 October. Available at: https://www.artribune.com/arti-visive/archeologia-arte-antica/2021/10/restauro-palazzo-silvestri-rivaldi-roma-collezione-torlonia/ (Accessed: 8 September 2023).

Han, J., Forbes, H. and Schaefer, D. (2021) "An exploration of how creativity, functionality, and aesthetics are related in design", *Research in Engineering Design*, 32, pp. 289–307. Available at: https://doi.org/10.1007/s00163-021-00366-9.

Hellqvist, D. (2010) "Hedi Slimane × Rolls Royce", *Dazed*, 9 April. Available at: https://www.dazeddigital.com/photography/article/7214/1/hedi-slimane-x-rolls-royce (Accessed: 25 July 2023).

Hess, L. (2020) "Everything you need to know about #GucciFest", *Re-edition*. Available at: https://www.reeditionmagazine.com/latest/everything-you-need-to-know-about-guccifest (Accessed: 25 July 2023).

Hypebeast (2019) "Moncler hosts a talk on the future of creativity with Hiroshi Fujiwara, Kevin Ma and Hans Ulrich Obrist", *Hypebeast*, 2 April. Available at: https://

hypebeast.com/2019/4/moncler-hiroshi-fujiwara-kevin-ma-hans-ulrich-obrist-event-recap (Accessed: 24 July 2023).

Hoang, L. (2021) "Virgil Abloh is the king of culture. Luxury wants in", *Luxury Society*, 11 August. Available at: https://luxurysociety.com/en/articles/2021/08/virgil-abloh-king-culture-luxury-wants (Accessed: 13 May 2023).

Holt, D.B. (2002) "Why do brands cause trouble? A dialectical theory of consumer culture and branding", *Journal of Consumer Research*, 29/1, pp. 70–90. Available at: https://doi.org/10.1086/339922.

Iley, S. (1984) "Corporate art collecting as a learning experience", *Business Quarterly*, 49/1, p. 8.

Imam, J. (2020) "First look at the Torlonia marbles, as the last great private collection of classical sculpture opens to the public", *The Art Newspaper*, 14 October. Available at: https://www.theartnewspaper.com/2020/10/14/first-look-at-the-torlonia-marbles-as-the-last-great-private-collection-of-classical-sculpture-opens-to-the-public (Accessed: 12 September 2023).

Itzkowitz, L. (2020) "Bulgari continues its epic Roman patronage with the priceless 'Torlonia Marbles'", *Architectural Digest*, 20 October. Available at: https://www.architecturaldigest.com/story/bulgari-torlonia-marbles (Accessed: 6 September 2023).

Jelinek, J.S. (2018) "Art as strategic branding tool for luxury fashion brands", *The Journal of Product and Brand Management*, 27/3, pp. 294–307. Available at: https://doi.org/10.1108/JPBM-01-2017-1408.

Khnychkin, Y. (2014) "One-on-one with Bulgari CEO Jean-Christophe Babin", *Haute Time*, 29 September. Available at: https://www.hautetime.com/one-one-bulgari-ceo-jean-christophe-babin/58926/ (Accessed: 22 September 2023).

Klamer, A. (2011) "Cultural entrepreneurship", *The Review of Austrian Economics*, 24/2, pp. 141–156. Available at: https://doi.org/10.1007/s11138-011-0144-6.

Knox, S. and Casulli, L. (2023) "Exploring founder identity tension, resolution, and venture pursuit", *Journal of Small Business Management*, 61/6, pp. 2488–2518. Available at: https://doi.org/10.1080/00472778.2021.1905821.

Koronaki, E., Kyrousi, A.G. and Panigyrakis, G.G. (2018) "The emotional value of arts-based initiatives: strengthening the luxury brand-consumer relationship", *Journal of Business Research*, 85, pp. 406–413. Available at: https://doi.org/10.1016/j.jbusres.2017.10.018.

Kottasz, R., Bennett, R., Savani, S. and Ali-Choudhury, R. (2008) "The role of corporate art in the management of corporate identity", *Corporate Communications*, 13/3, pp. 235–254. Available at: https://psycnet.apa.org/doi/10.1108/13563280810893634.

Lawry, C.A. and Helm, S. (2014) "Curating the creative genius in luxury firms", in B. Berghaus, G. Müller-Stewens and S. Reinecke (eds.) *The Management of Luxury: A Practitioner's Handbook*. London: Kogan Page, pp. 113–126.

LVMH (2019a) *Bvlgari Renews Support for Preservation of Rome's Cultural Heritage with Project to Restore Area Sacra di Largo Argentina Archaeological Site*, 5 March. Available at: https://www.lvmh.com/news-documents/news/bvlgari-renews-support-for-preservation-of-romes-cultural-heritage-with-project-to-restore-area-sacra-di-largo-argentina-archeological-site/ (Accessed: 12 October 2023).

LVMH (2019b) *Main Sponsor Bvlgari Contributes to Restoration of 96 Ancient Marble Statues from the Torlonia Collection*, 13 November. Available at: https://www.lvmh.com/news-documents/news/main-sponsor-bvlgari-contributes-to-restoration-of-96-ancient-marble-statues-from-the-torlonia-collection/(Accessed: 15 October 2023).

LVMH (2021) *LVMH 2021 Annual Report: Passionate About Creativity.* Available at: https://r.lvmh-static.com/uploads/2022/03/lvmh_rapport-annuel-2021-va.pdf (Accessed: 22 July 2023).

LVMH (2023) *Fondation Louis Vuitton.* Available at: https://www.lvmh.com/group/lvmh-commitments/art-culture/fondation-louis-vuitton-initiative-lvmh/ (Accessed: 16 October 2023).

Mansour, L. (2020) "Bulgari CEO Jean-Christophe Babin Talks Coronavirus, His Love for Italy and the Upcoming Plans for the Jeweller", *Aeworld*, 4 May. Available at: https://aeworld.com/watches-jewellery/watches/bvlgari-ceo-jean-christophe-babin-talks-coronavirus-his-love-for-italy-and-the-upcoming-plans-for-the-jeweller/ (Accessed: 7 September 2023).

Maserati (no date) *Fragment Design Special Edition: A Bold Operanera and Operabianca.* Available at: https://www.maserati.com/gb/en/brand/stories-of-audacity/fragment-design-x-maserati (Accessed: 24 July 2023).

Massi, M. and Turrini, A. (2020) *The Artification of Luxury Fashion Brands: Synergies, Contaminations, and Hybridizations.* London: Palgrave Macmillan.

Matten, D. and Crane, A. (2005) "Corporate citizenship: toward an extended theoretical conceptualization", *The Academy of Management Review*, 30/1, pp. 166–179. Available at: http://dx.doi.org/10.5465/AMR.2005.15281448.

Mazzucato, M. (2022) *Mission Economy: A Moonshot Guide to Changing Capitalism.* London: Penguin Books.

Milnes, H. (2017) "Forget see-now-buy-now: 2017's fix for the fashion calendar was collaborative projects", *Glossy*, 13 December. Available at: https://www.glossy.co/fashion-calendar/forget-see-now-buy-now-2017s-fix-for-the-fashion-calendar-was-collaborative-projects/ (Accessed: 7 June 2023).

Milnes, H. (2018) "The king of the collab: Virgil Abloh can seemingly do no wrong when it comes to partnerships", *Glossy*, 18 June. Available at: https://www.glossy.co/fashion/the-king-of-the-collab-virgil-abloh-can-seemingly-do-no-wrong-when-it-comes-to-partnerships/ (Accessed: 21 November 2022).

Morency, C. (2021) "From Virgil to the fashion world, and beyond", *Highsnobiety*, 20 July. Available at: https://www.highsnobiety.com/p/virgil-lvmh-off-white-louis-vuitton/ (Accessed: 16 August 2023).

Morency, C. (2022) "Suddenly it's about everything but the fashion", *Highsnobiety*, 21 October. Available at: https://www.highsnobiety.com/p/everything-but-fashion-content-luxury/ (Accessed: 5 June 2023).

Morency, C. and Obrist, H.U. (2020) "Raf Simons in conversation with Hans Ulrich Obrist: plotting an artistic future", *Highsnobiety*, 26 February. Available at: https://www.highsnobiety.com/p/raf-simons-x-hans-ulrich-obrist/ (Accessed: 9 May 2023).

Mouratidou, E. (2020) *Re-presentation Policies of the Fashion Industry: Discourse, Apparatus and Power.* London: Wiley-ISTE.

Muret, D. (2015) "Dolce & Gabbana patrons of Milan's La Scala opera house", *Fashion Network*, 15 December. Available at: https://uk.fashionnetwork.com/news/dolce-gabbana-patrons-of-milan-s-la-scala-opera-house,607803.html (Accessed: 3 September 2023).

OECD (2022) *The Culture Fix: Creative People, Places and Industries.* Paris: OECD Publishing. Available at: https://doi.org/10.1787/991bb520-en.

Parguel, B., Delécolle, T. and Mimouni Chaabane, A. (2020) "Does fashionization impede luxury brands' CSR image?", *Sustainability*, 12/1, 428, pp. 1–16. https://doi.org/10.3390/su12010428.

Pechman, A. (2015) "Max Mara's legacy of art patronage", *WSJ*, 30 April. Available at: https://www.wsj.com/articles/max-maras-legacy-of-art-patronage-1430422773 (Accessed: 17 April 2023).

Proctor, R.A. (2009) "The evolving marriage of art and fashion", *Luxury Society*, 6 April. Available at: https://www.luxurysociety.com/en/articles/2009/04/the-evolving-marriage-of-art-and-fashion (Accessed: 2 March 2023).

Qiu, B. (2019) "The art of selling luxury", *Frieze*, 26 June. Available at: https://www.frieze.com/article/art-selling-luxury (Accessed: 24 May 2023).

Reginato, J. (2019) "Rome welcomes Palazzo Rhinoceros, Alda Fendi's new cultural hub for the Eternal City", *Sotheby's*, 14 February. Available at: https://www.sothebys.com/en/articles/rome-welcomes-palazzo-rhinoceros-alda-fendis-new-cultural-hub-for-the-eternal-city (Accessed: 15 September 2023).

Riley-Smith, A. (2021) "A new dawn: in conversation with Yana Peel, Chanel's Global Head of Arts & Culture", *Vogue*, 19 May. Available at: https://www.voguehk.com/en/article/art-lifestyle/chanel-yana-peel-interview/ (Accessed: 7 June 2023).

Rolex (2023) *Rolex Mentor and Protégé Arts Initiative*. Available at: https://www.rolex.com/perpetual-arts/mentor-and-protege (Accessed: 28 September 2023).

Rudowicz, E. (2003) "Creativity and culture: a two way interaction", *Scandinavian Journal of Educational Research*, 47/3, pp. 273–290. Available at: https://doi.org/10.1080/00313830308602.

Rushford, A. (2023) "Moncler Genius brings immersive experience 'Art of Genius' with Adidas, Pharrell, Alicia Keys & more to London Fashion Week", *FN*, 6 February. Available at: https://footwearnews.com/2023/focus/collaborations/adidas-moncler-genius-london-fashion-week-experience-1203404501/ (Accessed: 7 June 2023).

Salessy, H. and Marain, A. (2021) "Off-White: 26 collaborations that brought Virgil Abloh to the forefront of the fashion scene", *Vogue France*, 29 November. Available at: https://www.vogue.fr/fashion/fashion-inspiration/story/off-white-the-18-collabs-that-cemented-virgil-ablohs-career/1635 (Accessed: 10 May 2023).

Salibian, S. (2021) "Armani Group becomes supporting founder of Teatro alla Scala Foundation", *WWD*, 26 April. Available at: https://wwd.com/feature/armani-group-supporting-founder-teatro-alla-scala-milan-1234810212/ (Accessed: 9 September 2023).

Santagata, W. (2004) "Creativity, fashion and market behavior", in D. Power and A.J. Scott (eds.) *Cultural Industries and the Production of Culture*. New York: Routledge, pp. 75–90.

Serafin, A. (2022) "Anthony Vaccarello launches his reimagined retail concept with the new Saint Laurent Rive Droite boutique", *Wallpaper*, 7 October. Available at: https://www.wallpaper.com/fashion/saint-laurent-rive-droite-boutique-retail-concept-anthony-vaccarello (Accessed: 4 August 2023).

Silver, H. (2022) "Van Cleef & Arpels' high jewellery ballerinas are an ode to dance", *Wallpaper*, 10 October. Available at: https://www.wallpaper.com/watches-and-jewellery/van-cleef-arpels-high-jewellery-ballerinas (Accessed: 25 November 2022).

Tauer, K. (2022) "Inside ICNCLST, the creative agency behind the most exciting artist-brand collaborations", *WWD*, 29 November. Available at: https://wwd.com/eye/people/

icnclst-sky-gellatly-creative-agency-artist-brand-collaborations-1235418663/ (Accessed: 9 June 2023).

Waddock, S. (2007) "Corporate citizenship: the dark-side paradoxes of success", in S.K. May, G. Cheney and J. Roper (eds.) *The Debate over Corporate Social Responsibility*. New York: Oxford University Press, pp. 119–134.

Weber, M. (2005) *The Protestant Ethic and the Spirit of Capitalism*. Translated by T. Parsons. London: Routledge. Available at: https://doi.org/10.4324/9780203995808.

Whitechapel Gallery (2023) *Max Mara Art Prize for Women*. Available at: https://www.whitechapelgallery.org/max-mara-art-prize-for-women/#:~:text=The%20Max%20Mara%20Art%20Prize,Mara%20Fashion%20Group%20in%202005 (Accessed: 2 October 2023).

Wong, J.Y. and Dhanesh, G.S. (2017) "Corporate social responsibility (CSR) for ethical corporate identity management: framing CSR as a tool for managing the CSR-luxury paradox online", *Corporate Communications: An International Journal*, 22/4, pp. 420–439. Available at: https://doi.org/10.1108/CCIJ-12-2016-0084.

Wood, D.J. (1991) "Corporate social performance revisited", *The Academy of Management Review*, 16/4, pp. 691–718. Available at: https://doi.org/10.2307/258977.

Yotka, S. (2020) "With a 'Show on the Wall,' Loewe delivers a jolt of fashion to your doorstep", *Vogue*, 1 October. Available at: https://www.vogue.com/article/loewe-spring-2021-show-on-the-wall (Accessed: 6 March 2022).

Zargani, L. (2019) "Fendi unveils four restored fountains in Rome", *WWD*, 26 November. Available at: https://wwd.com/feature/fendi-unveils-four-restored-fountains-in-rome-1203378686/ (Accessed: 6 March 2022).

Conclusions

This book has interrogated luxury brand and art collaborations within their wider socio-cultural context, analysing initiatives and crossovers through five specific thematic lenses – postmodernity, space, time, status and identity – drawing on seminal works in human science and more recent contributions to the phenomenon.

The resulting kaleidoscopic approach has enabled us to capture collaborations in their dynamic and multifaceted interaction with our consumption practices and experience. Whilst from a mere business standpoint the introduction of art-enhanced collaborations provides unique and enthralling outputs that counterbalance the volume issue of luxury production (Kapferer, 2015; Parguel, Delécolle and Mimouni Chaabane, 2020), in the broader context this reflects the current condition of the market, where consumer access to such enriched and spectacular products (Debord, 1994; Boltanski and Esquerre, 2020) has become an anchor for meaning in the midst of disaggregating socio-political institutions and the chaotic overflow of goods, images and contents. Rather than an unchanging, taken for granted relationship between art and luxury in a vacuum, luxury brand and art collaborations emerge here as a specific genre, both product and production of the postmodern consumption culture.

Looking at the defining features of luxury brand and art collaborations, the cases profiled evidence the level of complexity and sophistication they have reached over the years: collaborations are increasingly conceived as ensemble programmes, with one concept articulated into a range of products and activations across several touchpoints; they are rolled out through original or unconventional formats – spatial hackings, temporary installations, content festivals and videogames. In their quest to surprise and appeal, luxury brands engage with the heterodox aesthetics of countercultural art movements and source stories and icons from their own archives, which are artistically turned into immersive exhibitions for renowned cultural institutions around the world. The advance and application of digital technologies has further expanded the creative breadth of collaborations: art-infused digital tokens are sold or auctioned on crypto marketplaces, linked to physical purchases

DOI: 10.4324/9781003274094-7

or randomly drafted as prizes, which in turn gives rise to new dynamics of distinction among existing customers and new audiences.

These bountiful releases of collaborative initiatives are the result of the ceaseless, polymathic activity of individual and corporate actors across sectors and levels: brand creatives initiate spontaneous liaisons with artists while also getting involved in bona fide cultural projects, from spatial curations to solo artistic shows; artists apply their signature style to refresh luxury brands' product lines and enchant retail spaces, experimenting with new media and creative languages; besides supporting product-based commercial projects, brands invest into long-term partnerships with global art fairs and venture into cultural management by establishing mentoring programmes, art prizes and cultural foundations; under the helm of visionary CEOs, corporations innovate their business models and organisational practices to become creative incubators of capsule edits and media content such as podcasts and e-magazines. This provides solid ground to support the analysts' predictions according to which "by 2030, this industry will be drastically transformed. We will not talk about luxury industry anymore, but of the market for insurgent cultural and creative excellence" (D'Arpizio, in D'Arpizio and Levato, 2020).

Underpinning the cultural analysis of luxury brand and art collaborations is a Janus-faced view on postmodernity, mourning on the one hand the disappearance of the modern spatial-temporal coordinates, the liquified societal compass and the blurring lines of codified genres and aesthetics, and picking on the other through the debris to find new opportunities of expression and value (Firat and Venkatesh, 1995).

The debate about the hue of Jean-Michel Basquiat's *Equals Pi* included in Tiffany's "About Love" campaign and Jeff Koons' loose approach to the Old Masters in his collaboration for Louis Vuitton (Chapter 1) certainly evidence the lost relevance of factual authenticity and historical exegesis in favour of suggestive snippets of reality or empty simulacra (Baudrillard, 1994); at the same time, Nicolas Ghesquière's collection with Fornasetti and the *Re-signify* exhibition series by Pierpaolo Piccioli for Valentino (Chapter 3) highlight the semantic richness resulting from this bricolage work, which recomposes fragments from different geo-temporal contexts into a meaningful new whole. In actuality, the mix-and-match of genres, aesthetics and styles appears to be the only language to effectively convey the diasporic condition of minorities caught between belonging and rejection, as powerfully demonstrated by Virgil Abloh's *Peculiar Contrast, Perfect Light* catwalk show (Chapter 1).

Abloh applied his constructive take on postmodernity (Firat and Venkatesh, 1995) in confronting another aspect, i.e., the functional convergence between retail and cultural venues: the Church & State room in his *Figures of Speech* museal exhibition (Chapter 2) ironically deconstructs the boundary between aesthetic appreciation and consumption. Meantime, the K-11 Art Mall model in China (Chapter 4) deeply questions the intellectual legitimacy of this boundary, turning spatial hybridity into an act of cultural emancipation from Western-imposed constructs, and La Galerie Dior (Chapter 2) has ush-ered in a new spatial concept, a sensorial and imaginative ecosystem where museal vocabulary and brand storytelling are combined into a mesmerising experience.

Ephemeral projects, such as Prada's 24h Museum and the two-week-open-ing of Ruinart Hotel 1729 by Jonathan Anderson (Chapter 3), epitomise the temporal contraction of postmodern consumption desires. By the same to-ken, these and other instances – see also the one-night, by-invite-only Hermès Club and the livestreamed clubbing event in Cartier's "Make Your Own Path" (Chapter 4) – are actually capitalising on the intrinsic value of single moments to provide clients and audiences with an enhanced sense of exclusive access to luxury.

The continuous involvement of luxury companies in the art world has reconfigured their role from producers of products into stewards of culture, as in the case of Bulgari's Roman patronage or the Fondation Louis Vuit-ton by French conglomerate LVMH (Chapter 5). The criticism against corpo-rate funding of art brings back the modern view on the separation of private wealth from public good, calling us to reshape the relations between enter-prises and central governments instead of passively accepting the dominance of the neoliberal-capitalist market over socio-political institutions, typical of postmodernity.

We are currently entering a new historical phase, where our liquifying ex-istence has transcended into a different state: in the resulting "gaseous" set-ting (Morace, 2023), human beings are finally liberated from the structures, narratives and constrictions of modernity, yet find themselves suspended in a volatile reality where everything and everybody is at risk of becoming ir-relevant. In this capricious context, people strive to assert their ego rather than their social status, inflating their "iconographic power" (Morace, 2023, p. 84) on social media to attract likes and attention: here, the Debordian logic of the spectacle is interiorised at a personal level, with individuals offering themselves as spectacular products (Barile, 2017). Artificial intelligence and generative technologies are not merely providing society with tools to create new dimensions – as the Internet communication technologies had previ-ously done – but they are taking centre stage as independent producers of realities and contents, ultimately questioning human agency at its very core (Harari, 2023).

The challenge for gaseous individuals and civilisations is to fly with inten-tion, navigating through their rarefied condition with projects orbiting around sound principles – conscience, beauty, human and environmental dignity (Morace, 2023). It is in this evolving scenario that they will generate new ways of seeing luxury and art, their interaction and formalised partnerships, ultimately reinventing the paradigm of aesthetic and economic productivity, and its socio-cultural valence.

Bibliography

Barile, N. (2017) "Branding, selfbranding, making: the neototalitarian relation between spectacle and prosumers in the age of cognitive capitalism", in M. Briziarelli and E. Armano (eds.) *The Spectacle 2.0: Reading Debord in the Context of Digital Capitalism*. London: University of Westminster Press, pp. 151–165.

Baudrillard, J. (1994) *Simulacra and Simulation*. Translated by S.F. Glaser. Ann Arbor: University of Michigan Press.

Boltanski, L. and Esquerre, A. (2020) *Enrichment: A Critique of Commodities*. Translated by C. Porter. Cambridge: Polity Press.

D'Arpizio, C. and Levato, F. (2020) "How Covid-19 has accelerated the transformation in Luxury", *Bain & Company*, 9 December. Available at: https://www.bain.com/insights/how-covid-19-has-accelerated-the-transformation-in-luxury-video/?utm_source=Master+UK&utm_medium=email&utm_campaign=In+the+News(Accessed: 10 November 2023).

Debord, G. (1994) *Society of the Spectacle*. Translated by K. Knabb. London: Rebel Press.

Firat, A.F. and Venkatesh, A. (1995) "Liberatory postmodernism and the reenchantment of consumption", *Journal of Consumer Research*, 22/3, pp. 239–267. Available at: https://doi.org/10.1086/209448.

Harari, Y.N. (2023) "Yuval Noah Harari argues that AI has hacked the operating system of human civilisation", *The Economist*, 28 April. Available at: https://www.economist.com/by-invitation/2023/04/28/yuval-noah-harari-argues-that-ai-has-hacked-the-operating-system-of-human-civilisation?utm_content=section_content&gclid=Cj0KCQiAr8eqBhD3ARIsAIe-buOZCI70QYeEUeEG5Irfwig2gzF6Gbwku-GNFl8nYS2hZE2KXXYOfqoaAjfwEALw_wcB&gclsrc=aw.ds (Accessed: 7 November 2023).

Kapferer, J.N. (2015) *Kapferer on Luxury: How Luxury Brands Can Grow Yet Remain Rare*. London: Kogan Page.

Morace, F. (2023) *Modernità Gassosa: Istruzioni di volo contro la sindrome del pallone gonfiato*. Milano: Egea.

Parguel, B., Delécolle, T. and Mimouni Chaabane, A. (2020) "Does fashionization impede luxury brands' CSR image?" *Sustainability*, 12/1, 428, pp. 1–16. https://doi.org/10.3390/su12010428.

Index

For Product Safety Concerns and Information please contact our EU representative GPSR@taylorandfrancis.com
Taylor & Francis Verlag GmbH, Kaufingerstraße 24, 80331 München, Germany